# Elijah & Elisha

# The Holy Spirit and Christian Maturity

Ransom Press International embraces the ministry of the Holy Spirit as essential to Christian maturity and paramount to living a life victorious over sin, the world, and the devil. Unless we are directed by the indwelling presence of the Holy Spirit we have no hope of an inheritance with Christ. For all that are led by the Spirit of God, the same are sons of God (Romans 8).

As joint-heirs with Christ, we may receive of the Father's pleasure and promise, everything that Christ has received, including the anointing of the Holy Spirit. And by the Spirit we have gifts and ministry, yet these bear fruit through us in step with our desire to do things God's way, and not our own. Because of this, we see differences in gifts and ministry among the sons of God, for all come to maturity in their own time and according to their willingness to bear the cross of Christ. For this same reason we would not assume all manifest the same power and anointing, over a given course of time, yet we do expect that all will reach maturity with a powerful anointing.

It is with this in mind that our ministry focuses on preaching Christ at every level of belief and faith, being long-suffering with those who mature slowly, yet keeping pace to meet the need of those progressing from hearing to seeing by the Spirit. We favor neither group or denomination, one over another, nor do we produce Christian materials that promote a belief system other than the cross of Christ and all that is accomplished by it. We recognize the Holy Spirit as our sole covering and, therefore, our allegiance is neither to men nor organizations. However, we are ready and willing to cooperate with men and organizations where, by the Spirit, the same are ministering with pure hearts and clean hands. To preach the cross of Christ and accomplish the work of God to save souls from among all men—especially those who seem unlikely candidates for the kingdom of God.

At Ransom Press International our ultimate mission is for *the perfecting of the saints in the work of the ministry, unto the edifying of the body of the Christ until we all come forth in the unity of the faith and of the knowledge of the Son of God unto a perfect man, unto the measure of the coming of age of the Christ: That we no longer be children, tossed to and fro and carried about with every wind of doctrine, by the sleight of men and cunning craftiness, by which they lie in wait to deceive, but following the truth in charity, let us grow up into him in all things, who is the head, the Christ: From whom the whole body fitly joined together and well tied together among itself by the nourishment that every connecting bond supplies, by the operation of each member according to measure they have received, making increase of the body unto the edifying of itself in charity* (Ephesians 4:12–16).

# Elijah & Elisha

## The Mantle for God's People

**RUSSELL M. STENDAL**
Editor of the jubilee BIBLE

Elijah & Elisha
The Mantle for God's People
Russell M. Stendal
Copyright © 2016, 2019

All rights reserved. No part of this book may be reproduced, stored in a retrieval system, or transmitted in any form or by any means — electronic, mechanical, photocopying, recording, or otherwise, without written permission from the publisher.

Scripture quotations are taken from the Jubilee Bible, copyright © 2000, 2001, 2010, 2013
Russell M. Stendal.
All rights reserved.

Cover Art: *Matt Philleo*
Editors: *Donna Sundblad and Ruth Zetek*
Layout and cover design: *Martha Cecilia Jaramillo*

Printed in the United States of America

Ransom Press International
4918 Roosevelt Street
Holywood, Florida, 33021

Paperback ISBN: 978-0-93122-118-7
eBook ISBN: 978-0-93122-109-5

Available wherever books are sold

For questions or comments, visit:
https://ransompressinternational.com/contact-us/

Visit Russell's ministry website at:
https://cpcsociety.ca

RANSOM PRESS INTERNATIONAL

# Contents

Introduction ............................................................. 1

## Part I
### The Church Age is Closing

Chapter One ............................................................. 7
    Apostasy of Kings and the Church

Chapter Two ............................................................. 19
    The Altar and the Gospel

Chapter Three .......................................................... 35
    The Still, Small Voice

Chapter Four ............................................................ 47
    King Ahab Goes from Bad to Worse

Chapter Five ............................................................. 61
    Naboth's Vineyard

Chapter Six .............................................................. 71
    The Defeat of King Ahab is the Tipping Point

## Part II
### The New Day in God Is Dawning

Chapter Seven .......................................................... 85
    Elijah Enters the Realm of Total Victory

Chapter Eight ........................................................... 97
    The Double Portion

Chapter Nine ............................................................ 117
    The Way Out of Edom and the Defeat of Moab

Chapter Ten ............................................................. 133
    The Sons of the Prophets

**Chapter Eleven** ............................................................................................. 143
    God Heals Naaman, the Enemy General

**Chapter Twelve** ............................................................................................. 155
    Seeing from God's Perspective

**Chapter Thirteen** ........................................................................................ 165
    The Tribulation is Unexpectedly Cut Short

**Chapter Fourteen** ....................................................................................... 171
    A Spiritual Famine

**Chapter Fifteen** ........................................................................................... 183
    Jezebel's Downfall

**Chapter Sixteen** .......................................................................................... 195
    Baal Worship Is Eradicated out of Israel

# Introduction

Over the past sixteen years, I preached almost one thousand spontaneous messages through the Bible (a chapter or so per message) for the various radio stations God placed in our path to manage and program.[1]

Several years ago the Lord impressed my spirit to translate at least one hundred of these messages into English and to publish them. The completion and publication of this book brings the total of translated messages to ninety-nine, with the sixteen chapters found in this book coming from original radio messages preached before a live audience at Salón Los Héroes in Bogotá.

****

Bible prophecies often overlap to a certain degree. This is true of most of the prophetic books including Revelation. To make prophecy less confusing, think of these overlaps as snapshots of a future event taken from different angles. Each one offers a bit of new detail and perspective.

God uses prophecy to deliver his message on multiple levels — to an individual or a nation, and in some cases, to reveal end-time events. The natural and the spiritual realms are linked and as you will see in this book, a lot of action is about to take place on both sides of the veil (1 Corinthians 15:46).

The books of the first half of the Old Testament include narrative that on the surface doesn't seem to be overtly prophetic. However, this book will show that it contains often-overlooked surprises, including passages found in First and Second Kings. And while the Old Testament is ripe with these messages, for this book I have narrowed the focus to portions pertaining to the ministries of Elijah and Elisha.

---

[1] You may download the free App Jubilee Radio from the iTunes store to listen to our English radio signal (In Spanish the App is Fuerza de Paz).

Please note that 2 Kings chapters 3-10 undoubtedly overlap to some extent and present different facets of the same truth from different angles. It may be confusing to think of this prophetically as a straight chronology. Also, the years that the different kings from Israel and from Judah were in power sometimes seem a bit out of sync. Bear in mind that, particularly with Judah, King David set a precedent when he proclaimed Solomon king *before* his death. This could also have happened in the transition from Jehoshaphat to Jehoram (as well as others). Similarly, the dating for the reigns of the kings is often plus or minus one year for reasons such as counting the first and final years as full years, even if the king reigned for less than twelve months. So, if you add the total years of the kings of Israel and compare this with the total of the kings of Judah, the two sums aren't the same due to such factors.

It is amazing that the spectacular prophetic ministries of Elijah and Elisha took place in the midst of the apostate kingdom of Israel and not in Judah. Elijah is only mentioned once in the book of 2 Chronicles (which likely was written by the scribes and priests at the temple in Jerusalem). Yet it is at the darkest and most corrupt time in history that God's prophets really shine. And it is remarkable how much love, mercy, and miraculous opportunity God poured out upon wicked kings and an apostate people who abused his name. In the center of all of this, we find the ministries of Elijah and Elisha. This inspires hope for the present situation of God's people, as we are also in the midst of a very dark and corrupt hour.

God's judgment is about to fall upon Israel and the church in a way similar to what happened in Israel to Jezebel and the worshippers of Baal and the house of Ahab, in the days of Elijah and Elisha. The tares are about to be removed from among the wheat (Matthew 13:30, 38).

The account written in First and Second Kings is there for our benefit and admonition.

> Now all these things happened unto them as types, and they are written for our admonition, upon whom the ends of the ages are come. (1 Corinthians 10:11)

## Introduction

Truly a new day in God is before us. For those whose hearts are pure, this new day will bring unprecedented opportunity to reach out with a double portion of the unfailing love of God, even to our worst enemies. I am a witness to the victorious power of the love of God. Time and time again I've not only been miraculously delivered from my enemies, but they have also come and made peace with me (Proverbs 16:7).

I've been able to stand firm and prevail unscathed in the midst of every type of trial and turmoil imaginable. What I have witnessed and experienced convinces me more than ever that the message in this book is true — we are in the midst of the prophetic fulfillment of the story of Elijah and Elisha.

> Charity [the love of God] is never lost, but prophecies shall come to an end, tongues shall cease, and knowledge shall come to an end. For we know in part, and we prophesy in part.
>
> But when that which is perfect is come, then that which is in part shall be done away. When I was a child, I spoke as a child, I understood as a child, I thought as a child; but when I became a man, I put away childish things.
>
> For now we see as through a mirror, in darkness, but then we shall see face to face; now I know in part, but then I shall know even as I also am known. And now abide faith, hope, charity, these three; but the greatest of these is charity. (1 Corinthians 13:8-13)

# Part I
# The Church Age is Closing

# Chapter One
## Apostasy of Kings and the Church

First Kings 16 describes a twelve-year period of prosperity, palace intrigue, and ever-increasing apostasy in the northern kingdom of Israel. Judah also experienced decay and corruption at this time but to a lesser degree. In this type of environment, power, opportunity, and prosperity accelerated the effects of corruption like yeast in a lump of dough.

In some ways, this parallels the history of the church as well as the trajectory of the United States with God's many attempts throughout human history to have a "clean" people. Those who founded the United States sought freedom to follow the Lord according to conscience. They found freedom along with adversity, and in our nation's history there were at least three times when God touched the entire nation. During this Great Awakening, it is estimated that over half of the U.S. population coast to coast was converted.

As with Israel in the book of 1 Kings, our nation hasn't really been on track with God for at least four generations, while the effects of corruption continue to rise in a geometric progression. Something evil is going on in America that is different from the problems in Colombia and many other parts of the world. America has people who don't want to know anything about God. In fact, they desire to do away with anyone who mentions God. Their goal is to persecute and extinguish even the memory of God (Romans 1:19-32).

Israel, and later Judah, was at a similar place culturally. They reached the point that even if they happened to have a "good" king, he was unable (or unwilling) to do anything about the demonic culture being imposed. For example, when good King Asa of Judah was under pressure from Baasha, king of Israel, he didn't seek the

Lord with all his heart. Instead, he took money from the house of the Lord and hired an enemy—King Benhadad of Syria—to attack Israel (1 Kings 15:18-22). Why? Because his vision and his faith (even with a good heart) were very weak. He no longer believed he could face things in the name of the Lord. As a result, he didn't even ask: What does God think?

It seems to me that we have many people like this in the world today. They seek solutions to problems they see, and they even claim to believe in God, but in reality, they don't have much faith.

It is in a similar environment of almost total spiritual darkness that we come to King Ahab of Israel who,

> did evil in the sight of the LORD above all that were before him ... and he took to wife Jezebel, the daughter of Ethbaal, king of the Zidonians, and went and served Baal and worshipped him. (1 Kings 16:30-31)

Baal is the god of prosperity of this world. This is the principle problem within the church and the United States today with many eager to have their ears tickled with the "prosperity gospel."

## 1 Kings 17

> ¹ Then Elijah, the Tishbite, who was of the inhabitants of Gilead, said unto Ahab, As the LORD God of Israel lives, before whom I stand, there shall not be dew nor rain these years, but according to my word.

Elijah came seemingly out of nowhere and with no genealogy. We know nothing of his background or training. Because of this lack of credentials, Ahab may not have taken him seriously at first. Soon, however, Elijah had Ahab's undivided attention. Notice the judgment he proclaimed didn't deal in hours, days, weeks, or months. It is a judgment of years:

> As the LORD God of Israel lives, before whom I stand, there shall not be dew nor rain these years, but according to my word. (v. 1)

This wasn't the first time God dealt with mankind in this way. Think of Adam and Eve. They lost their standing before God and were expelled from his presence, and mankind has lived in this tragic state for the past six thousand years. At the time when Elijah delivered God's prophecy to Ahab, Israel (the people of God) was already generations into such serious apostasy that it would prove terminal for the northern kingdom.

In 1 Kings we see a prophetic voice come abruptly on the scene—a voice sent from the direct presence of God. This verse offers an example of the multi-faceted aspect of prophecy I spoke about in the introduction of this book. It not only applied to what was happening in Israel at the time, but is also prophetic regarding future events (Malachi 4:5; Luke 1:17) relating to the first and second coming of Jesus Christ.

Israel had gone from bad to worse until Elijah, whom the LORD delegated, confronted the most evil king they had ever had. After Elijah delivered God's warning that there would be no rain or dew until God gave the word, he disappeared from the sight of the king and everyone else. The heavens were shut up for three years and six months in accordance to the word he delivered, while he remained steadfast, even though he was despised in Israel (Luke 4:24-25).

In the Scriptures, the word of a true prophet of God always remains firm, unlike many who pass for prophets among the people of God today who *claim* a large percentage of their "prophecies" come true. Those who write horoscopes in the newspapers can also claim a similar degree of accuracy. The fact is that Scripture says a true prophet of God must be one hundred percent accurate. Not one word can fail (Deuteronomy 18:20-22). This was the case with Moses, Samuel, Elijah, and with the Lord Jesus. And *the testimony of Jesus is the spirit of prophecy* (Revelation 19:10). True prophets can be very unpopular.

Elijah was sent by God, seemingly out of nowhere in the time of Israel's darkest hour. Elijah didn't mess around. His message wasn't superficial. Look one more time at the message he delivered.

> As the LORD God of Israel lives, before whom I stand, there shall not be dew nor rain these years, but according to my word. (v. 1)

Dew and rain represent the Word and the revelation of the Lord in Scripture.

> Behold, the days come, said the Lord GOD, that I will send a famine to the earth, not a famine of bread, nor a thirst for water, but of hearing the words of the LORD: and they shall wander from sea to sea, and from the north even to the east, they shall run to and fro to seek the word of the LORD, and shall not find it. (Amos 8:11-12)

## 1 Kings 17

> ² And the word of the LORD came unto him, saying,
>
> ³ Leave this place and turn to the east and hide thyself by the brook Cherith, that is before the Jordan,
>
> ⁴ and thou shalt drink of the brook, and I have commanded the ravens to feed thee there.

Is the raven a clean bird? No. It is an unclean scavenger.

> ⁵ So he went and did according unto the word of the LORD; for he went and dwelt by the brook Cherith, that is before the Jordan.
>
> ⁶ And the ravens brought him bread and flesh in the morning and flesh in the evening, and he drank from the brook.

Where did the ravens get the bread and flesh?

> ⁷ And it came to pass after a while that the brook dried up because there had been no rain in the land.
>
> ⁸ And the word of the LORD came unto him, saying,
>
> ⁹ᵃ Arise, go to Zarephath of Zidon, and thou shalt dwell there.

God sent Elijah out of the Promised Land. Zarephath means "place of refining."

> ⁹ᵇ Behold, I have commanded a widow woman there to sustain thee.

This widow woman wasn't an Israelite; she was in Zidon, which means "fishing."

¹⁰ So he arose and went to Zarephath. And when he came to the gate of the city, behold, the widow woman was there gathering of sticks; and he called to her and said, Bring me, I pray thee, a little water in a vessel, that I may drink.
¹¹ And as she was going to fetch it, he called to her again and said, Bring me also, I pray thee, a morsel of bread in thy hand.
¹² And she said, As the LORD thy God lives, I have no baked bread, but only a handful of meal in a pitcher and a little oil in a cruse, and now I was gathering two sticks that I may go in and prepare it for me and my son, that we may eat it and die.
¹³ And Elijah said unto her, Fear not; go and do as thou hast said, but first make me a little cake of bread baked under the ashes and bring it unto me, and afterwards thou shalt make for thee and for thy son.
¹⁴ For thus hath said the LORD God of Israel, The pitcher of meal shall not be consumed, neither shall the cruse of oil fail until that day when the LORD shall send rain upon the earth.
¹⁵ And she went and did as Elijah told her; and he and she and her house ate for many days.
¹⁶ And the pitcher of meal was not consumed, neither did the cruse of oil fail, according to the word of the LORD which he spoke by Elijah.

He did all this in the house of a pagan widow who sustained the prophet Elijah, until the Lord sent rain upon the earth. For many of us, the Lord has strategically placed someone in our lives to sustain us in a similar fashion when we've had nothing or seemed weak. God provided through this widow. She supplied Elijah's need, according to the Word of the Lord at a time in history when the blessing wasn't supposed to be for the Gentiles. This would be like using a non-Christian today.

Many tell us that it's not the right time or dispensation for God to act, but the prophet Haggai prophesied that the right time is when the Lord says (Haggai 1:2-11). Paul wrote to Timothy and encouraged him to be ready in season and out of season. Why? Because even if it isn't the right time for others, it may be the right time for us.

When we are told it's not the right time or season for God to use us, or we aren't in the right dispensation, that we must wait, or God used people in the past and will do many wonderful things in the future, but now isn't the right time, we must always remember: the right time is when God says.

The helpless, starving widow was God's provision for Elijah. God moved the prophet and at the same time prepared the widow. Then things got even more interesting:

> ¹⁷ And it came to pass after these things that the son of the woman, the mistress of the house, fell sick; and his sickness was so severe that there was no breath left in him.
> ¹⁸ And she said unto Elijah, What have I to do with thee, O thou man of God? Art thou come unto me to call my iniquity to remembrance and to cause my son to die?
> ¹⁹ And he said unto her, Give me thy son. And he took him out of her bosom and carried him up into the chamber where he abode and laid him upon his own bed.
> ²⁰ And he cried unto the LORD and said, O LORD my God, hast thou even brought evil upon the widow, with whom I sojourn, by killing her son?
> ²¹ And he stretched himself upon the child three times and cried unto the LORD and said, O LORD my God, I pray thee, let this child's soul come into him again.
> ²² And the LORD heard the voice of Elijah, and the soul of the child came into him again, and he revived.
> ²³ And Elijah took the child and brought him down out of the chamber into the house and delivered him unto his mother, and Elijah said, See, thy son lives.
> ²⁴ Then the woman said to Elijah, Now by this I know that thou art a man of God and that the word of the LORD is true in thy mouth.

The priests down at the temple took great care to protect their holy things. If anything unclean touched an item, it became contaminated. Even their sacrifices, the meat of their offerings — which was sacred to God — became unclean if it touched anything unclean (Haggai 2:13). This is the case with everything relating to the religion of men. Everything can become easily contaminated.

God began something new with Elijah, which had the possibility to increase and spread. Elijah gave rise to Elisha, and Elisha desired and discovered how to receive a double portion of what Elijah had. Elijah and Elisha are examples for all of us, but this is nothing in comparison with our Lord Jesus who isn't limited to a double portion. He has boundless resources and unlimited anointing. Right now, he is seated at the right hand of the Father with all authority, with all power, and with no limits.

Whatever he touches, no matter how unclean or contaminated, no matter how dead, can revive and live. When he places his hand upon someone, he can leave that person clean and alive even though at the beginning they were dead and unclean.

We are very close to a spiritual tipping point in history, and in order to go where we need to go, we need a direct encounter with the life of God. God has a new day on the horizon. The day of man has moved from bad to worse. All sorts of intrigues of power and corruption have intermingled among the people of God — corruption that will continue to grow and fester, until it is confronted with the life of God.

The prophet Elijah not only stopped the blessing (rain) from God upon the perverted religious system of his day, he also began something new — something initiated by God. The parallels for our present day and age are incredibly exciting. Very little about Elijah was *kosher* according to the established religion of Israel. Think about it. First, unclean ravens fed him, and then a Gentile widow sustained him.

According to the Law, nothing about him was clean. But what made all of this clean and acceptable to God (ravens, Gentile widow, camel's-hair cloak, unclean food, etc.) was the genuine life of God within Elijah. He truly lived in the presence of God. Elijah had something others didn't have — direct access to God. When God declares someone clean, they are really clean (Acts 10:15). The Gentile widow woman actually said: *Now by this I know that thou art a man of God and that the word of the LORD is true in thy mouth* (1 Kings 17:24).

When Jesus passed by a funeral procession, he went over and touched the corpse, and the young man came back to life (Luke 7:12-15). Touching the dead was unthinkable for the Jews. If they touched a corpse, it made them unclean and required a long, complicated process in order to be cleansed.

I have encountered "messianic" Jews who refuse to even consider that Jesus would do such a thing, because they lack the faith and vision to see what Jesus showed by his example. Instead, they think the gospel account is in error — that Jesus, as a pious Jew, would never have contemplated touching a corpse or leper. When Jesus touched the corpse, instead of him becoming unclean, the corpse revived to life. This was a sign pointing to who he is and that his Word is true.

When Elijah brought the pagan widow lady's son back to life, she wasn't concerned with religious rules or labels. Instead, when her son came back to life, it was infallible proof that she had a genuine man of God under her roof, and the Word of the LORD in his mouth was true.

In our present-day culture, we have a religious sphere where everything that touches the life of the natural man becomes contaminated — unclean and dead — a place among the sons of Adam, void of the life of God. Many put on a false impression of being religious and pretending that they have something: they dress in a certain manner, speak with religious vocabulary, and attend solemn rituals. Some have spectacular buildings and beautiful music. Many live as if it is acceptable to be religious on the outside while living a lifestyle of hidden sin.

The reality is that they can't really cleanse anything with such actions. Jesus compared people like this to whitewashed tombs, beautiful on the outside while rotten and corrupt on the inside. Everything they touch becomes contaminated, not just in church and not just in religion. Everything touched by the natural man in the economic realm or concerning government and society in general is corrupted. All of this will continue on its present disastrous course until confronted by the true presence of God.

God desires to place his presence *in* us. He desires to reveal an end-time Elijah company, for the anointing of Elijah to become the double portion of Elisha and for all of this to introduce us to the unlimited realm of Jesus Christ, until Christ becomes all and in all (Colossians 3:10-11).

Elijah means "the LORD is God." Elisha means "God of the coming (one)." John the Baptist is typed with Elijah (Matthew 11:14). Elisha is typed with the coming One (Jesus Christ). Scripture states that end-time events will be *as in the days of Noah* (Luke 17:26), which leads us to the question: What was going on in the days of Noah?

Those days were, in fact, very similar to the description of what was taking place in Israel in 1 Kings 15 and 16 and also parallel to what is presently happening in places like Bogotá, Miami, and other places all over the world today. Corruption will grow worse until it is confronted with the life of the Lord — life he desires to place into people like us, into those who corporately make up the body of Christ.

If we are at a crossroads — a turning point in history — when God desires to effect a major change, we may see it more clearly in the days ahead as we look back. Indicators show we are rapidly approaching a historic moment in which the Lord will place a small remnant to stand and confront the present corruption. This remnant may include some of us.

Scripture doesn't indicate that Elijah had an impressive background or education or that he was a proven leader. Nothing. All we know for sure is his name: Elijah the Tishbite (meaning stranger) who was of the inhabitants of Gilead (meaning hill of the testimony).

Elijah didn't come forward on his own initiative. An alternate interpretation of the name Elijah is "God Himself." Elijah said that he stood before the LORD. He had access to the presence of God. This trumps everything else.

What we do and say on our own will have no tangible effect on the crazed and enraged world around us. In order to combat the corruption, someone who is clean in God's eyes and who will do and say only what God wants is required. Jesus said that it's not necessary for us to prepare what we are going to say in advance. He promises to give us the right words at the proper time (Matthew 10:19).

When the Lord decides it is the right time, some of us will be involved in a head-on collision with the corrupt system of this world. Scripture declares that the day of the LORD shall begin with gloom and darkness. At first, things will appear completely hopeless, but later there shall be light.

The first time I returned to the U.S. after 9/11, all the security at airports and the borders amazed me. These all-out attempts were made to keep out potential terrorists, but looking at this from a spiritual point of view, we've already been invaded by demonic enemies.

Only a small remnant of people filled with the presence of God is left. The situation is far gone, and we are spending huge sums of money on security and defense in the natural realm while our spiritual defenses are almost completely breached.

The most serious problem we face in Colombia isn't the guerrillas, the paramilitary, the narcos, or even the common delinquents. The real problem in Colombia is centered in each corrupt heart, whether it is found in school children, college students, politicians, or anyone else. The sad fact is that the real problem is centered in the hearts of almost everyone.

As long as we seek to solve the problem in any place other than our hearts, we will continue in defeat. We need to understand that the first priority, as far as the Lord is concerned, is to cleanse our hearts.

God may use those with a pure heart as he desires. Being used of God isn't difficult. It doesn't require a diploma or degree, nor does our age limit our effectiveness for God. Paul reminded Timothy of this when he told him,

> Let no man despise thy youth, but be thou an example of the faithful in word, in conversation, in charity, in spirit, in faith, in purity. (1 Timothy 4:12)

God is about to do things no one has ever seen before — to use people who, in the eyes of many, would never amount to anything. When he decided to shake things up in Israel, he brought someone on the scene no one knew anything about — a guy who lived on a remote mountain (located outside the borders of their realm). This man announced the only credentials he needed. He said in effect, "I come from the presence of God!"

They had never seen Elijah, until the day he stood before King Ahab in the middle of the worst evil mess in the history of the nation of Israel and announced,

> As the LORD God of Israel lives, before whom I stand, there shall not be dew nor rain these years, but according to my word. (v. 1)

In the New Testament, we learn Elijah was a man like us. He prayed and God heard him (James 5:17). Elijah didn't have to raise his voice or even repeat himself. When I read this, you know what I think? I think many, many people pray today who aren't being heard. Even with numerous and repetitious prayer meetings, God doesn't seem to respond in the way he consistently responded to Elijah. In fact, many prayer meetings of today have more in common with the prophets of Baal.

Jesus said the pure in heart shall see God (Matthew 5:8). A pure heart trumps religiosity every time. The pure in heart will be intimately involved with God as he unveils his special plans. If, at the time of opportunity we refuse to receive his Word and don't allow him to awaken his Spirit in us, then the opportunity won't be for us. It will be for others. I am convinced that we stand at the threshold of a great opportunity. Even if I am mistaken about end-time events, if you follow the advice I offer in this book, it will do you good.

If we have allowed the LORD to cleanse our hearts, the time will come when God will work through us in ways that may seem off base or even crazy to others. However, if you allow God to cleanse you, he will use you. This is what happened with Elijah — a down-to-earth, common person like any of us.

**Let us pray:**

Lord, we ask that this example may be clear, that we may understand that your life and what you consider to be clean is very different from what is taught by the religion of men.

May we understand the importance of having pure hearts so we may have unlimited vision to go forward wherever you send us. Amen.

# Chapter Two
## The Altar and the Gospel

### 1 Kings 18

*¹ And it came to pass after many days that the word of the LORD came to Elijah in the third year, saying, Go, show thyself unto Ahab; and I will send rain upon the earth.*

Many references to the third day or the third year can be found in Scripture. For instance, Jesus said he would be resurrected on the third day. The number three refers to life, resurrection, and restoration. The Word of the LORD came to Elijah in the third year of a tremendous drought. With that in mind, let's consider the following:

We are presently entering the third millennium (or third prophetic day) since the first coming of the Lord Jesus. Our situation hasn't been that wonderful up until now. We still have numerous people worshipping God and the god of worldly prosperity (Baal) at the same time. They seek their own pleasure and try to keep God happy at the same time. This mirrors the situation taking place in the days of Elijah and King Ahab.

*² And Elijah went to show himself unto Ahab. And there was a severe famine in Samaria.*

Remember that not even one drop of rain or dew had fallen in years. In the same way, the church has languished in a spiritual drought for a very long time. Historians look at all that happened in the early church and try to explain the impotence of the modern church by saying conditions were very different back then. Some theologians think we've experienced the silence of God since the death of the first century apostles! Others who have mixed the gospel of prosperity—the gospel of Baal—with the gospel of Jesus Christ are in the midst of a flurry of seemingly supernatural activity. This reminds us once again to reconsider the prophecy of Amos that talks about a *famine to the earth, not a famine of bread, nor a thirst for water, but of hearing the words of the LORD* (Amos 8:11).

Many today invent their own word of faith. Others unite with a person, organization, or movement instead of to the Lord. Those who hear directly from the Lord are scarce. Even for those who have the privilege of attending meetings where the preacher hears from God, the blessing is limited. Unless each person hears directly from the Lord, they won't receive the grace to fulfill the will of God.

> ³ And Ahab called Obadiah, who was the governor of his house. (Now Obadiah feared the LORD greatly,
>
> ⁴ for when Jezebel cut off the prophets of the LORD, Obadiah took one hundred prophets and hid them in groups of fifty in caves and sustained them with bread and water).

Obadiah (servant or worshipper of the LORD) feared the Lord but didn't have direct contact with him. Elijah, on the other hand, not only feared the Lord but also had direct contact with the Lord—a big difference.

> ⁵ And Ahab said unto Obadiah, Go through the land to all the fountains of water and to all the brooks; peradventure we may find herbage to save the horses and mules alive that we not lose all the beasts.

Deuteronomy 17:16 warns that the kings of Israel weren't to multiply horses for themselves. Solomon and others rebelled against this directive, and the consequences led to the serious famine of Elijah's day. And note that even though people were in danger of starvation, the foremost priority on the mind of Ahab was to not lose all his beasts.

In Scripture *beasts* can be symbolic of humans who walk according to the flesh. Ahab, meaning "father's brother" (uncle), wanted to believe in God but also wanted to seek everything the world had to offer. Today we call such people carnal Christians. In fact, this is why Ahab married Jezebel and why he allowed her to keep all those false prophets.

True prophets were extremely scarce but so was green grass! Ahab's beasts were in danger of starvation. Spiritually this meant the famine was so bad it was interfering with Ahab's ability to walk after the flesh. The same end-time scene is also described in Revelation 8:7 when the first trumpet is blown and all the green grass is destroyed.

> ⁶ So they divided the land between them to pass throughout it; Ahab went one way by himself, and Obadiah went another way by himself.
>
> ⁷ And as Obadiah was in the way, Elijah met him; and when he recognized him, he fell on his face, and said, Art thou not my lord Elijah?
>
> ⁸ And he answered him, I am; go, tell thy lord, Behold Elijah [Heb. The LORD is God].
>
> ⁹ And he said, In what way have I sinned that thou should deliver thy slave into the hand of Ahab, for him to slay me?

When Obadiah met Elijah along the way, he feared Elijah would disappear and that Ahab would kill him for not arresting the prophet. For many years, no one cared much for the true prophets of God. Obadiah had hidden two groups of fifty persecuted prophets in caves. Fifty is the number representing pentecost, and the Feast of Pentecost is representative of the church age over the past two prophetic days (one thousand years per day, 2 Peter 3:8) in the midst of severe spiritual famine. Through all this time, many servants of the LORD, like Obadiah, have feared the Lord but lacked the direct personal fellowship and intimate communion with God the Father. Obadiah continued:

> ¹⁰ As the LORD thy God lives, there is no nation or kingdom where my lord has not sent to seek thee; and when they all said, He is not here; he has caused kingdoms and nations to swear an oath if they have found thee or not.
>
> ¹¹ And now thou sayest, Go tell thy lord, Behold Elijah.

¹² And it shall come to pass as soon as I am gone from thee, that the Spirit of the LORD shall carry thee where I know not; and so when I come and tell Ahab, and he cannot find thee, he shall slay me; but I, thy slave, fear the LORD from my youth.

¹³ Was it not told my lord what I did when Jezebel slew the prophets of the LORD, how I hid one hundred men of the LORD's prophets in groups of fifty in caves and sustained them with bread and water?

This type of action has occurred throughout much of church history with true prophets being run out by Jezebel and her false prophets. On many occasions, true prophets were "hidden" and given "bread and water." In Obadiah's case, he thought hiding the prophets was a grand accomplishment, while he also served and catered to Ahab and Jezebel's every whim.

¹⁴ And now thou sayest, Go, tell thy lord, Behold Elijah; and he shall slay me.

Note that Obadiah also wanted to protect his own life. He was the governor of the palace in Israel, which was supposed to be the people of God. And, yes, he feared God and *secretly* helped God's prophets, but he wasn't even willing to contradict Ahab, let alone Jezebel.

How many times have we seen leaders of large religious groups who do more or less as they please, riding rough shod over the true people of God? In these congregations, administrators or assistants who truly fear God often worry about the consequences if they should contradict the leader(s). Those like Obadiah think they are doing a great service to God by helping to maintain a few true prophets of God on bread and water over in some hidden cave on the mission field.

¹⁵ And Elijah said unto him, As the LORD of the hosts lives, before whom I stand, I will surely show myself unto him today.

Why did Elijah decide to show himself to Ahab on this day? Because it was God's time.

Historically we are coming to the moment in time when God will confront those who have placed themselves as kings over the people of God. I don't believe God will use a single individual for this task. He has prepared an entire army — an Elijah company, if you please.

> 16 Then Obadiah went to meet Ahab and told him, and Ahab came to meet Elijah.
>
> 17 And it came to pass when Ahab saw Elijah, that Ahab said unto him, Art thou he that troubles Israel?
>
> 18 And he answered, I have not troubled Israel; but thou and thy father's house, in that ye have forsaken the commandments of the LORD, and thou hast followed Baalim.

Baal is the god of prosperity — the god of the grand preachers who preach that if you follow their message, you will receive the best of *this* world, and heaven to boot! Vast multitudes enjoy hearing these sermons while only handfuls, like Obadiah, fear the Lord but don't know where else to go because the kings of the large groups have completely dominated the people of God.

So Elijah said unto Ahab:

> 19 Now therefore send and gather to me all Israel unto Mount Carmel; and the four hundred and fifty prophets of Baal and the four hundred prophets of the groves, who eat at Jezebel's table.
>
> 20 Then Ahab sent unto all the sons of Israel and gathered the prophets together unto Mount Carmel.

Carmel means "fruitful garden." God intends for his people to be like a fruitful garden, but the consequences of doing things man's way produces the opposite effect and leaves them dry and barren.

> 21 And Elijah came near unto all the people and said, How long shall ye halt between two opinions? If the LORD is God, follow him; but if Baal, then follow him. And the people did not answer him a word.

²² Then Elijah spoke again unto the people, I, even I only, remain a prophet of the LORD; but Baal's prophets are four hundred and fifty men.

²³ Give us, therefore, two bullocks, and let them choose one bullock for themselves and cut it in pieces and lay it on wood and put no fire under it; and I will dress the other bullock and lay it on wood and put no fire under it.

²⁴ And invoke ye in the name of your gods, and I will invoke in the name of the LORD; and it shall be that the God that answers by fire is God. And all the people answered and said, It is well spoken.

²⁵ So Elijah said unto the prophets of Baal, Choose you one bullock for yourselves and dress it first, for ye are many, and invoke in the name of your gods, but put no fire under it.

Baal means "master or lord" but plural.

²⁶ And they took the bullock which was given them, and they dressed it and invoked in the name of Baal from morning even until noon, saying O Baal, answer us. But there was no voice nor anyone that answered. And they jumped up and down near the altar which they had made.

²⁷ And it came to pass at noon that Elijah mocked them and said, Cry aloud, for he is a god; peradventure he is talking or he had to go to the latrine, or he is on a journey, or he sleeps and will awake.

²⁸ And they cried aloud and cut themselves after their manner with knives and lancets until the blood gushed out upon them.

²⁹ And when midday was past, even so they prophesied until the time of the offering of the evening sacrifice, and there was neither voice nor anyone that answered nor anyone that heard.

³⁰ Then Elijah said unto all the people, Come near unto me. And all the people came near unto him. And he repaired the altar of the LORD that was broken down.

This reflects the problem we have almost everywhere in Christendom: the altar of the Lord is in ruins. To better understand how this pertains to us, we must understand what the altar represents.

The Old Testament altar is the equivalent of the gospel in the New Testament. The altar represented sacrifice and God's conditions under which he could receive us, for we aren't acceptable on our own. It pointed to the perfect sacrificial Lamb, and today the only way God receives us is in the life of the Lamb of God, our Lord Jesus Christ. Work we do in our own strength, even religious work, isn't adequate or even acceptable. Our life must be placed into his hands. We must turn from our own course to head in his direction and follow him in faith.

If we are to go God's way, our own works must come to an end. We must be cleansed by him and do what he desires. This is completely opposite of what we were doing before.

The way of the Lord is not a wide path. It is a narrow way, and sometimes, at least at the beginning, it doesn't seem that pleasant. It is the way of the cross, a way that calls us to die daily to anything God doesn't like in us. As the old man is put to death, the new man in Christ will thrive.

The gospel says, *What shall it profit a man if he shall gain the whole world and lose his own soul?* (Mark 8:36).

So God's altar must be repaired.

> 31 And Elijah took twelve stones, according to the number of the tribes of the sons of Jacob, unto whom the word of the LORD came, saying, Israel shall be thy name;

*Israel* is the name of God, and the name symbolizes God's desire to place his very nature inside of his true people.

> 32 and with the stones he built an altar in the name of the LORD; then he made a trench round about the altar, as great as would contain two measures of seed.

The altar, symbolic of the death of the Lord Jesus, has enough room for all who are willing to surrender their lives to Jesus Christ. Jesus didn't die for us so we could continue to do whatever we please. No!

Jesus, in faithful obedience to his Father, died to show us the way (for he is the way), and he desires to take us down the same path he walked. This way leads to the true blessing of God through the death of the old man and the old nature. The blessing is only found in the life of Christ; it can only be fully entered if the old man is done away with.

Obadiah, the governor of the house of Ahab, hid one hundred prophets in caves, but at the moment of the supreme confrontation, none of those prophets appeared on the scene. In contrast, the prophet whom *God* hid emerged on the scene at the right moment. Isn't this interesting?

Often people ask God to bless what they are doing instead of doing what God is blessing. Things people say they do in the name of the Lord, but do with unclean hearts and motives, will come to naught. If we aren't clean before the Lord, things we are convinced were of God or for God and right to do, will amount to nothing. If we are clean, if the Lord has sent us, if the Lord has placed us where we are, and if we continue to be faithful to him even in very small things, then nothing will be able to move us if he doesn't want us to be moved. If we are involved in something that originates from the heart of God, then the Lord will maintain it. That which will remain and amount to something is that which flows from the heart of God.

The Lord desires to incorporate us into what he is doing — starting at the altar. The two measures of seed Elijah placed in the trench around the altar are symbolic of us. Within each of us is something that must die in order for God to be able to multiply the life of Jesus in and through us. Jesus said that unless the seed falls into the ground and dies, it cannot grow and be multiplied.

[33] And he put the wood in order ...

What does the wood represent? Wood is symbolic of our own good works. They must all be placed on the altar of God.

[33] *and cut the bullock in pieces and laid it on the wood ...*

Everything concerning our carnal walk dominated by the flesh must be surrendered upon the altar. Living in this manner will never even occur to those who follow the gospel of prosperity and worship over in Ahab's palace.

> ³³ and said, Fill four pitchers with water and pour it on the burnt sacrifice and on the wood.
>
> ³⁴ And he said, Do it the second time, and they did it the second time. And he said, Do it the third time, and they did it the third time.

Twelve pitchers of water were poured over the sacrifice. The number twelve is related to divine order, and water is symbolic of the Word of God. When we emphasize the ways of God and saturate everything we do with his Word, when the wood and the flesh and the seed are immersed in the abundance of water, one thing is for certain: there will be no false fire (Leviticus 10:1-2).

We aren't to be running around playing with matches attempting to spark a revival. This is an important lesson. The Lord doesn't send us to light the fire. It's not about creating a great event or filling a stadium by promising supernatural miracles in order to kindle a revival. God is the only one who can ignite a new work. The Lord will light the fire at the right time, and it might not be according to how or when we think it should happen. Elijah insisted on pouring more and more water upon the altar.

> ³⁵ So that the water ran round about the altar, and he had filled the trench also with water.
>
> ³⁶ And it came to pass at the time of the offering of the evening sacrifice that Elijah the prophet came near and said, LORD God of Abraham, of Isaac, and of Israel, let it be known this day that thou art God in Israel and that I am thy slave and that I have done all these things at thy word.
>
> ³⁷ Answer me, O LORD, answer me, that this people may know that thou art the LORD God and that thou shalt convert their heart back again to thee.

This is the ongoing problem with those *claiming* to be the people of God who need a true conversion of the heart.

Only three Scriptures in the Bible mention the God of Abraham, Isaac, and Israel. Most references mention the God of Abraham, Isaac, and Jacob. Why would this be?

Jacob was a conniver — an unconverted Israel. He represents someone who hasn't been converted but who uses the name of God for personal gain. God allowed himself to be named the God of Abraham, Isaac, and Jacob, but Scripture also shows the desire of his heart to convert Jacob. However, Jacob wasn't easy to convert. In order for this to be accomplished, Jacob had to pass through a period called the time of Jacob's trouble.

Only when Jacob thought he would lose everything and be killed did he desperately seek the Angel of the LORD. He fought all night with the LORD and refused to let go unless he was blessed. In order to bless him, God had to damage Jacob's walk in the flesh. Jacob left with the blessing and with a name from God — Israel. And he limped for the rest of his life (Genesis 32:24-32).

God isn't willing that any should perish (2 Peter 3:9). He has plans for everyone. Great personalities of today, like Ahab, may soon experience the time of Jacob's trouble with all of their followers. They will either fight for or against God. If Jacob had continued to resist God, for even a little bit longer, he might not have prevailed. The Angel told him clearly that time was running out, and he would leave before morning.

Elijah also knew he was in a serious struggle and that time was running out. He desperately requested an answer from God so *that this people may know that thou are the LORD God and that thou shalt convert their heart back again to thee* (v. 37).

This is the only hope, because if God's people aren't transformed from the inside out, what hope is there for those who are out in the world? Our main problem isn't the devil or the demons or even terrorists or other enemies. No! The main problem is that most of the people of God, in Israel and in the church, don't reflect a converted heart and, therefore, history repeats itself.

Not many are like Elijah, though we have plenty who are like Obadiah who do things they think are very good. Yes, Obadiah hid one hundred prophets (in two groups of fifty) and fed them bread and water, but where were those prophets when God sent Elijah to confront the prophets of Baal?

## 1 Kings 18

> 38 Then fire of the LORD fell, which consumed the burnt sacrifice and the wood and the stones and the dust and licked up the water that was in the trench.

Peter prophesied that,

> the heavens were created of old and the earth standing out of the water and in the water, by the word of God; by which the world that then was, being overflowed with water, perished;
>
> but the heavens, which are now, and the earth are conserved by the same word, kept unto the fire in the day of judgment and of perdition of the ungodly men. (2 Peter 3:5-7)

The entire world system will be destroyed when the Lord sends the real judgment by fire, prophesied by Peter (2 Peter 3). In the account of Elijah and the fire that came down from heaven, the sacrifice was consumed in a supernatural way. The sacrifice represents everything pertaining to our walk in the flesh. It will be consumed along with the wood, which represents our own good works. But what about the stones? Or the dust?

Man is made from the dust of the earth and will return to dust. We might assume the dust and stones, representing the divine order of God, would be fireproof, but something very interesting is about to happen. God is about to change the fundamental order of many things.

The day of man? The order of pentecost? Twelve sons of Jacob or of Israel? Twelve apostles? No, no, no, and no. The Lord is about to do something that will fulfill the prophecy about having only one shepherd and one sheepfold (John 10:16).

In another place the prophecy states that even key persons like Noah, Daniel, and Job would only be able to save themselves and no one else (Ezekiel 14:14-20). Why? We are coming into a time when only those who have a direct personal relationship with God will be saved.

It won't be enough to be under pastors or elders or leaders who hear the voice of the Lord and use God-given gifts in leadership of a flock, which is dependent upon the leader(s). No!

People must have their own link directly to God the Father and be under his discipline.

The order established in Israel and in the church will all go up in smoke when the fire of God comes down. We can make preparations like Elijah did. We can preach messages, distribute Bibles, and do many other good things as long as the Lord directs us to continue to pour "water" upon the sacrifice. It is very important to remember that everything Elijah did was according to the Word of the LORD.

When the fire fell, one of the most important things that happened was that the real fire of God once again burned upon the altar of God. If God's presence isn't at the altar and the Lord doesn't intervene directly in the heart of each person, no one can do anything to rectify the situation. What good would it do for someone to have a Bible and to listen to us preach if the fire of the conviction of the Spirit of God doesn't sweep them away?

The true presence of God wipes out all of the opposition. We don't control the true presence of God, and it isn't confined by man-made limits or structures.

## 1 Kings 18

> [39] And seeing it, all the people fell on their faces, and they said, The LORD, he is the God; the LORD, he is the God.

The people didn't fall on their backs; they fell on their faces. When the true fire of God falls once again, the people will fall upon their faces. In Hebrew, when they said, *The LORD, he is the God* — it sounded like saying *Elijah!*

God chose Elijah to represent him. This is what is lacking in so many places today. God desires to have representatives who represent him according to his wishes and desires.

⁴⁰ And Elijah said unto them, Seize the prophets of Baal; let not one of them escape. And they seized them; and Elijah took them down to the brook Kishon and slew them there.

Why did he kill them? You might be thinking *poor prophets! Why not give them a nice little Sunday school class?*

He killed them because they had spent a very long time prophesying their false prophecies in Israel, and the deception they propagated caused the eternal loss of many people eternally in Israel. Their deception placed the entire nation in grave danger.

Jesus said that when he returns and finds wicked servants causing trouble in his house, he will destroy those wicked servants and replace them with those found faithful (Luke 20:16).

⁴¹ Then Elijah said to Ahab, Go up, eat and drink; for there is a sound of abundance of rain.

The prophets of Baal had to be destroyed in order for the blessing to flow upon the people of God once again. Rain is symbolic of blessing.

⁴² So Ahab went up to eat and to drink. And Elijah went up to the top of Carmel, and he cast himself down upon the earth and put his face between his knees

⁴³ and said to his slave, Go up now, look toward the sea. And he went up and looked and said, There is nothing. And he said, Go again seven times.

⁴⁴ And the seventh time he said, Behold a little cloud like the palm of a man's hand arises out of the sea. And he said, Go and say to Ahab, Prepare thy chariot and descend that the rain not stop thee.

I have seen preachers interpret the little *cloud like the palm of a man's hand* to mean that a hand has five fingers, and these hypothetical fingers must represent the fivefold ministry of apostles, prophets, evangelists, pastors, and teachers who, according to them, need to move in and take immediate control of any new revival. That isn't necessarily true. We must be very careful to not misinterpret Ephesians 4:11-16.

This little cloud was the size of the palm of a man's hand but says nothing about fingers. It really represents a very small beginning, and God will have *his* hand on this new thing, which will quickly spread into a major storm. According to the book of Revelation, there will be lightning, thunder, and hail. We're not talking light rain.

> ⁴⁵ *And it came to pass in the meanwhile that the heavens became black with clouds and wind, and there was a great rain. And Ahab rode and went to Jezreel.*

Jezreel means "God plants" or "God scatters." For many years during the church age, human ministry has dominated the people of God. Man has done a lot of planting but hasn't produced lasting fruit, because he hasn't had the true blessing of God. The fullness of the blessing of God cannot fall upon the old man.

We have seen that when believers allow the old man to reign, even with gifts and ministries of God, they can never be completely blessed. Within the church, we've had exemplary men and women of God, but as a whole the church hasn't entered into the fullness of the blessing. Now God is going to plant, and we will see a huge difference.

> ⁴⁶ *And the hand of the LORD was upon Elijah, who girded up his loins and ran before Ahab to the entrance of Jezreel.*

It doesn't say that Elijah, as a great prophet, is one of the fingers of the hand of God. It says that the hand of the LORD was upon Elijah. Under the hand of the LORD, Elijah was able to outrun the horses of Ahab's chariot, because God had warned the kings of Israel not to trust in horses (and therefore not to trust in chariots drawn by horses), which represent the flesh and the religious machinery of man (Deuteronomy 17:16). When the hand of God moves us, we can outperform any religious organization unequally yoked to man.

God will soon light things on fire once again. When the true fire of God falls, several possibilities become viable.

First, the false prophets will be revealed for who they really are, and they will lose their power. The fire of God will prepare the way for each individual to have a direct encounter with the presence of God so they may be led directly by him. When the fire of God falls, every false religious structure will eventually come apart and disappear.

For this reason, I haven't had the heart or desire to foment a private kingdom or to do things I see being done in other places "because they work." We aren't going to twist arms and take up offerings to construct a religious fortress and fill it with offices for people to come and seek counsel from us. No sir! All of these organizations are very soon going to become like Solomon's temple or like Herod's temple: not one stone will be left upon another.

The only thing that will remain firm in the day of the Lord is the personal relationship with him. There will be one shepherd and one sheepfold (Ezekiel 34:23; John 10:16). There is only one mediator between God and men, and we know who he is. No one can touch him because he is seated at the right hand of the Father with all power and authority to mediate the New Covenant as he sees fit.

We are finishing 2000 years of New Covenant practice according to the ways of man and look where we are! We aren't much better off than Israel under King Ahab. We are presently in one of the most corrupt moments of church and world history.

Where are we going?

The Lord will join those who are pure in heart, those who have allowed him to cleanse their hearts. We don't need to have an important position in this world. We only need to allow the Lord to work in our hearts, so he might cleanse us. Then he will also be able to work through us and to unite us with everyone else who has a pure heart.

Soon, and apparently out of nowhere, he will cause his kingdom to become visible. His kingdom has remained invisible, but soon he will cause it to appear. When it becomes visible, what will be seen? Us — if we belong to him, if we have allowed him to cleanse our hearts, if we have allowed him to work in and through us.

**Let us pray:**

Lord, we give you thanks for this example, for this message, for what we may learn and appropriate. We ask that we might be able to better understand your heart, your mercy towards us and that we might also understand what you desire from us so we might focus in the right direction.

May we seek your goals and your wisdom. Amen.

# Chapter Three
## The Still, Small Voice

### 1 Kings 19

¹ And Ahab told Jezebel all that Elijah had done and of how he had slain all the prophets with the sword.

² Then Jezebel sent a messenger unto Elijah, saying, So let the gods do to me, and more also, if by tomorrow at this time I have not made thy person as one of them.

³ And when he saw that, he arose and departed to save his life and came to Beersheba, which is in Judah, and left his servant there.

⁴ But he himself went a day's journey into the wilderness and came and sat down under a juniper tree; and desiring to die, he said, It is enough; now, O LORD, take away my life, for I am not better than my fathers.

Elijah showed strength and courage by facing the eight hundred and fifty false prophets of Baal when the Lord sent fire from heaven, and he was able to destroy all of them, but he took off running from Queen Jezebel.

When faced with adversity, the natural inclination of many Christians is to take off running. Over the past fifty years or so, many individuals and even entire groups have fled to other countries or remote wilderness areas, because they fear what is happening in the church and in the United States. However, when we fail (and especially if our mistake was an honest mistake), God does not fail. He will set up another opportunity for a victory that will be even more glorious, if we are willing to put our own lives on the altar. We may be refined so that under pressure we will continue doing things God's way no matter what.

It is interesting to note in 2 Kings that Elisha and those included in the school of prophets he mentored never had the slightest inclination to attempt to save their own lives. They were able to stand victorious in the midst of all of the intense perversion, corruption, and evil. Their fearless attitude was both victorious and contagious. This undoubtedly has a lot to do with the double portion of the Spirit of Elijah (of God Himself) that Elisha desired and obtained.

Jezebel represents the false prevalent religious system. Jezebel was the pagan daughter of Ethbaal, the king of the Zidonians, who married the king of Israel. King Ahab might not have remained as evil if not for the influence of Jezebel. He had opportunities and even repented on occasion during the course of his life; however, the strong sway of his wife caused Ahab to seek wrong goals. On the other hand, this same woman had a different effect on Elijah. She caused him to face reality about himself and uncovered his latent desire to save his own life. Sooner or later every Christian must face this reality.

Those who listen to the voice of prophets telling them that Israel or the United States or the church are hopelessly lost and they must flee to some supposed safe haven in another country or remote wilderness area need to ask themselves one thing. Why? Why are they attempting to retreat from the ongoing battle? Is it due to a desire to save their own lives or have they truly and personally heard from the LORD? Are they being led by him instead of reacting out of fear to the many religious (demonic) voices attempting to absorb their time and resources, so they lose their effectiveness for God?

There is a time to fight and a time to run, but Elijah so regretted running away from the battle with Jezebel that he asked the LORD to take his life.

The system represented by Jezebel doesn't just seek to do away with the prophets of God; it invades the people of God and contaminates them. It controls them from inside and uses Israel and the church (the people of God) to eradicate or banish all true prophets and all true worship (which is in Spirit and in truth). If you do not believe me just pack a suitcase full of Bibles or New

Testaments along with a few hundred excellent gospel tracts and go to the center of Jerusalem or Tel Aviv and pass them out. You will receive a very irate reaction from "Jezebel" almost immediately. Many churches (especially the big ones) are equally paranoid. Some have such a personality cult going on with the pastor that they receive no outside speakers. Period!

Therefore, prophets and others who flee such circumstances out of fear of corrupt man will most likely find that when they flee physically, wherever they go, their enemy will always be there, because the enemy has wormed its way inside of them. Jezebel does some of her best work from the inside, and most people don't consider this. This is why God requires the actual death of the old man (of the old carnal Adamic nature), before he will pour out the double portion of the fullness of our actual inheritance in Christ in the realm of the holy of holies. And only those commissioned directly from the realm of the throne of God have total victory.

What tool does Jezebel use? She uses the worship of Baal (the god of the prosperity of this world), which is indelibly linked to fornication. To understand better what this means, let's take a closer look at Baal.

Baal relates to the god of this world. The word Baal actually means "lord" (plural) and includes Satan and all of his demons, as they attempt to operate among the people of God as angels of light. Baal promises the prosperity of this world. A central part of Baal worship involves fornication, which includes adultery (Matthew 5:32), incest (1 Corinthians 5:1), and idolatry (2 Chronicles 21:11), and all types of sexual impurity.

The name Jezebel means "she does not cohabit (with her husband)." She seeks promiscuous relationships (spiritual and otherwise) with both men and women. If she can get God's people to seek the prosperity of this world, she can infiltrate their thoughts with the lie that it is possible to serve both God and Baal at the same time. She promises the best of this world and heaven too! Soon those duped by her promises are spiritually contaminated, completely defeated, and in total bondage to the flesh, the world, and the devil. The spirit of Jezebel operates in both men and women and changes the dynamics of entire groups.

Jezebel also specializes in duping religious people who believe in austerity. Even though they think they have totally rejected the world, Jezebel fools them into attempting to save their own lives and the lives of their families by embracing a strict, rustic, or communal lifestyle in some remote corner of this world. Jezebel is expert at finding and glamorizing ways to bypass the way of the cross. She doesn't just seduce those who are carnal; she's also creative in seducing those who consider themselves to be spiritual.

God says, *friendship of the world is enmity with God* (James 4:4). Those who are friends of the world are labeled adulterers and adulteresses. Why? The spirit behind this world is the enemy of God. Those who seek the things of this world (and even those who attempt to save their lives in this world instead of being willing to risk everything for the Lord) seek an alliance with another spirit — with another god that isn't the true God. This is spiritual adultery, and it produces spiritual bastards who claim the church as their mother; yet God is not their father. Receiving our spiritual directives and theology from one another instead of from the Spirit of God (who obviously also works through men and women of faith) is spiritual homosexuality. It is always sterile and fails to produce converts with transformed lives.

> Therefore, I beseech you brethren, by the mercies of God, that ye present your bodies in living sacrifice, holy, well pleasing unto God, which is your rational worship.
>
> And be not conformed to this age, but be ye transformed by the renewing of your soul that ye may experience what is that good and well pleasing and perfect will of God. (Romans. 12:1-2)

The Lord is very jealous. He won't permit his people to be with another god. He compares his relationship with his people to a marriage and requires fidelity and cleanliness. This is why the enemy's attack attempts to make the hearts of the people of God go astray.

First, he endeavors to get God's people to seek their own safety and security. Then he tempts them to seek after their own comfort. Finally, he lures the people of God to go after the things and goals of this world (remember that the love of money is the *root* of all evil). This opens the door to sexual and spiritual impurity, which also exposes the next generations to all sorts of perversion and abuse. The pagans were famous for brutally sacrificing their children to demons, and many parallels exist in our modern society. It isn't just those who fall to obvious worldly temptations who are prone to lose their children; those who fall on the opposite side of the horse into religious legalism are equally prone to lose their children.

Elijah came to realize he had underestimated Jezebel, and he was completely exhausted.

## 1 Kings 19

⁵ And as he lay and slept under a juniper tree, behold, then an angel touched him and said unto him, Arise and eat.

⁶ Then he looked and behold, there was a cake baked on the coals and a cruse of water at his head. And he ate and drank and went back to sleep.

⁷ And the angel of the LORD came again the second time and touched him and said, Arise and eat, for there is a great journey before thee.

⁸ And he arose and ate and drank and went in the strength of that food forty days and forty nights unto Horeb, the mount of God.

It may be necessary for us to spend some time in the "wilderness" in order to sort things out and overcome temptation. Elijah spent forty days and forty nights in the wilderness. The disobedient children of Israel spent forty years wandering in the wilderness until the whole unbelieving generation died off (a year for every day of disobedience after they refused to believe God and enter into the Promised Land). Remember that the wilderness we face may be spiritual or physical or both (Numbers 14:34; Deuteronomy 1:2-3; Revelation 12:14).

This is the same place where Moses received the Ten Commandments in the midst of forty days of fasting. Jesus, led by the Spirit, fasted for forty days in the wilderness and was ministered to by angels.

Elijah had a long journey. True fasting is a lifestyle; it is a daily denial of self (Isaiah 58). The only (spiritual) nourishment we must take in is what is provided by the Lord. Elijah's wilderness consisted of a trackless desert, which he traversed seemingly alone. Yet we may walk with Jesus if God has his hand on us (even though we may not see him) where there is no way, because he is the way, the truth, and the life. At the end of the journey, he was convinced he was completely alone both physically and spiritually in his prophetic ministry, even though the hand of God was still upon him.

Throughout history many excellent men and women of God have felt alone in much the same way, as they lick their wounds following an unsuccessful battle with Jezebel. In my travels, I find many who feel like this, because they haven't found even one person in their same town or city that they can share their life with in close fellowship. They haven't found a church or group or fellowship where they feel free of the domination, control, and perversion of Jezebel. Why is this?

The Lord is doing something different and preparing us for something unlike what we've experienced in the past. In the past, we could follow the Lord in our own life and seemingly be successful with the gifts, ministries, and direction God provided for us. It even seemed possible we could continue like this indefinitely, complemented by those congregated around us.

Let's face it — very gifted, dynamic individuals have the ability to minister in a big way, and some of it seems very real. But in the midst of all of this ministerial activity, somehow things keep getting tainted ever so slightly with Baal worship — the worship of the things and values of this world — starting with an obsession to save our own lives.

This worship results in people with tremendous gifts from God, who have great ministries that outwardly appear very successful, but they don't experience victory within. Instead, they struggle with things like fear, lust, and other wrong desires. They find themselves in troubled marriages and having problems with their children. In other words, they are beset with trouble on all sides.

To understand what the Lord is doing now, it is important to realize that as believers our relationship with him is of paramount importance. Consider this a vertical relationship between us here on earth and God in heaven. Our relationships with other people on earth can be looked at as horizontal in nature. The Lord is not in a hurry to horizontally join people together. Those who are deeply in tune with him (giving top priority to that vertical relationship) aren't in a rush to do so either. Why? Because we live in a time when God wants to join those whose hearts are pure and clean.

Sometimes he makes an exception and includes those who desperately desire to be clean but who still have a long way to go. However, the Lord desires an uncontaminated message to flow and for those who receive this message to experience God dealing directly with them. This encounter with God will affect their entire life, because the Lord not only desires clean hearts, he also desires the old man dead. We have a choice between Adam and Christ.

We will face difficult circumstances and attacks, until we are willing, like Elijah, to place our lives upon the altar, so God can do as he pleases. Even after we lay our lives down, we may experience difficult circumstances, but if that vertical link with God dominates, we will be eager to go wherever he desires. If he desires us to march through a lonely desert, then we will go through the desert. If it is a long journey, it doesn't matter. We'll go wherever he says. We will feed only upon what he provides; for *man shall not live by bread alone, but by every word that proceeds out of the mouth of God* (Deuteronomy 8:3; Matthew 4:4).

Those who seek their own comfort and gain won't do this. I'm talking about those who seek God, so he will do what they want, as if he were a genie who will prosper them in what they have determined to be a blessing. Such people will never embark on a journey knowing they may never return.

What does the Lord desire? He desires a clean people.

We already know that after leaven (corruption) sets in, even a little leaven leavens the entire lump. Therefore, we shouldn't be trying to see how many people we can embrace in our fellowship. It's not about numbers, focusing on numbers will result in bringing in the wrong people.

The gifts and ministries of God are given so we may enter into the life of Jesus Christ and bear good fruit under the discipline and chastening of our Heavenly Father. If gifts and ministries are used for personal (or even corporate) gain, the effect and purpose of God won't be fulfilled. This is what we see all around us. This is what Jezebel foments when her ways take root inside the people of God.

Back in 1 Kings, God is about to show Elijah how to defeat Jezebel. Some profound changes are required. In this passage, Elijah has just arrived at the mountain of God after travelling forty days and forty nights through the desert.

## 1 Kings 19

⁹ And there he went into a cave, where he lodged; and the word of the LORD came to him, and he said unto him, What doest thou here, Elijah?

¹⁰ And he replied, I have been very jealous for the LORD God of the hosts, for the sons of Israel have forsaken thy covenant, thrown down thine altars, and slain thy prophets with the sword; and I, even I only, am left, and they seek me to take my life.

¹¹ And he said, Go forth and stand upon the mount before the LORD. And, behold, the LORD passed by, and a great and strong wind rent the mountains and broke in pieces the rocks before the LORD, but the LORD was not in the wind.

¹² And after the wind an earthquake, but the LORD was not in the earthquake. And after the earthquake a fire, but the LORD was not in the fire. And after the fire, a still small voice,

> ¹³ᵃ Which when Elijah heard it, he covered his face in his mantle and went out and stood in the door of the cave.

This is the first time Elijah's mantle is mentioned. Elijah knew he was in the direct presence of God and this would normally kill a mortal man. Therefore, he went out and stood in the door of the cave but covered his face with his mantle (the mantle being a symbol of his being redeemed and covered by God).

> ¹³ᵇ And, behold, there came a voice unto him, saying, What doest thou here, Elijah?
>
> ¹⁴ And he replied, I have been very jealous for the LORD God of the hosts because the sons of Israel have forsaken thy covenant, thrown down thine altars, and slain thy prophets with the sword; and I, even I only, am left, and they seek me to take my life.

The Lord repeated the question, and Elijah gave the same answer. Why would the Lord ask the question the second time? It is because the Lord is looking for integrity and cleanness on the inside. If we don't hear and understand the still, small voice, then the wind and the earthquake and the fire will make no difference. This is why the glory of God has rapidly dissipated from the great revivals known throughout the history of the church. The rushing wind, earthquake, and fire of the upper room, of the Reformation, of the Great Awakening, and of subsequent revivals have withered into end-time apostasy in many places.

We won't be able to break free from the clutches of Jezebel by following past models for revival. Our only way out is to listen for the still, small voice and do exactly what God is telling each of us to do now, 24/7. This voice tends to speak in our hearts rather than in our minds.

> ¹⁵ And the LORD said unto him, Go return on thy way by the wilderness of Damascus; and thou shalt arrive there and anoint Hazael to be king over Syria;
>
> ¹⁶ and Jehu, the son of Nimshi, thou shalt anoint to be king over Israel; and Elisha, the son of Shaphat of Abel-meholah, thou shalt anoint to be prophet in thy place.

> ¹⁷ And it shall be that he that escapes the sword of Hazael, Jehu shall slay; and he that escapes from the sword of Jehu, Elisha shall slay.
>
> ¹⁸ And I will cause seven thousand to remain in Israel, all the knees which have not bowed unto Baal, and every mouth that has not kissed him.

The Lord promised Elijah he would cause seven thousand who hadn't bowed to Baal to remain in Israel. God's faithful remnant remains today even in the most corrupt venues of Israel and the church.

> Even so then at this present time also, there is a remnant by the gracious election of God. (Romans 11:5)

In the next chapter of Kings, we'll see a remnant of seven thousand face a much larger army and win. The only thing that can guarantee victory is if we keep our hearts on the altar before the Lord, so he can work from within us according to his good pleasure. If we enter wholeheartedly into what the Lord is doing, instead of trying to insert the Lord into our plans, the Lord will cleanse us. If we are in him, and he has cleansed us, guess what will happen?

He will join us with others who are clean and use us however he sees fit. As God joins us to others who are clean, he builds unity among his people — unity the enemy cannot break apart. This is why the Lord gives this promise:

> And I will cause seven thousand to remain in Israel, all the knees which have not bowed unto Baal, and every mouth which has not kissed him. (v. 18)

Seven represents completeness, and one thousand is symbolic of perfection. Seven thousand means all those who are walking in perfection (same word as maturity). The Lord will cause them to remain victorious in Israel. Israel means "the people of God." Only the Lord can walk in perfection, but he desires to do it in us. This is the only path to maturity in Christ.

> ¹⁹ So he departed from there and found Elisha, the son of Shaphat, who was plowing with twelve yoke of oxen before

> him, and he with the twelfth. And Elijah passed by him and cast his mantle upon him.

As I said earlier, twelve is a number that represents divine order. Elisha was obviously a faithful, hard worker on his father's farm, just as David had lived as a faithful shepherd. God has a habit of choosing those who are faithful in the natural realm when it is time to delegate spiritual responsibility.

In this story, Elijah's mantle, or covering, plays an important role. Elijah's commission came directly from the LORD with no intermediator. God told him to anoint Elisha to be prophet in his stead. From the very beginning, Elijah indicated that Elisha was being redeemed and called to be directly under the authority of God. For this reason, his submission to Elijah had to be voluntary. This is emphasized during Elisha's training. Elisha wasn't anointed to take Elijah's place until later, when he received the famous double portion.

The mantle worn by the prophet was made of camel's hair (the camel is an unclean animal). We have already seen that many aspects of Elijah's God-ordained lifestyle and diet didn't comply with the law. The New Testament Scripture states that those who are led by the Spirit aren't under the law. Elijah pioneered this concept.

> 20 So he left the oxen and ran after Elijah and said, Let me, I pray thee, kiss my father and my mother, and then I will follow thee. And he said unto him, Go back again, for what have I done to thee?

Elijah must have cast his mantle upon Elisha and then kept on walking (or maybe even running). Elisha spontaneously ran after Elijah and accepted the call of God. Elisha didn't have time to reason this out or even pray. He went with the impulse of his heart and asked only to kiss his father and mother goodbye, not to ask their permission. This indicates that Elisha was possibly more than thirty years of age (a symbol of maturity). There are similarities between the call of Elisha and the call of Jesus's disciples.

²¹ And he returned back from him and took a yoke of oxen and slew them and boiled their flesh with the instruments of the oxen and gave unto the people and they ate. Then he arose and went after Elijah and served him.

The pure in heart shall see God. The pure in heart will never be ashamed, confused, or defeated. The pure in heart won't only have the clarity of God, they will also have the grace to fulfill the will of God victoriously.

When others stand as conduits between the Lord and us, such as mentors, elders, clergy, or other intermediaries, and if we must receive our direction and revelation secondhand, the result is that we lack the grace and power to live a clean life and to have a victorious ministry.

Elijah received his direction and instruction directly from God, and Elisha was clearly on the same path. True God-ordained ministry seeks to join the people directly to the Lord.

### Let us pray:

Heavenly Father, we ask for clarity in the midst of so much confusion all around us, in the midst of so much enemy deception.

May we have the clarity to know that we can place our lives directly into your hands, that we can be made clean and pure no matter what the cost, so that we may be clean and useful in your kingdom.

We ask this in the name of our Lord Jesus Christ. Amen.

# Chapter Four
## King Ahab Goes from Bad to Worse

### 1 Kings 20

¹ Then Benhadad, the king of Syria, gathered all his host together; and there were thirty-two kings with him and horses and chariots; and he went up and besieged Samaria and warred against it.

Samaria was not Jerusalem. It was the capital of the ten tribes of Israel, which had separated from Judah and Benjamin when Jeroboam rebelled against Rehoboam, the son of Solomon. At this time Jeroboam started his own religion, which included his counterfeit version of the Feast of Tabernacles. His feast was celebrated in the eighth month rather than the seventh month, like God's feast. He incorporated his own altars and golden calves in Bethel and Dan. With such practices in place, the kings of Israel ruled the people in the midst of great deception and apostasy with Ahab being the most evil among them.

Jeroboam's actions were to Israel what the apostasy of Rome and Constantinople were in church history. Both set the stage for brutal wars and, in the case of the church, led to the Crusades and the Spanish Inquisition (among many other disasters).

Israel had enough of a connection to God that the enemy desired to get rid of them, but they lacked the full measure of grace from God to be well protected. Many in Israel and the church are in a similar situation today.

Ahab had occasional tendencies to want to please God, but he had a serious, fundamental problem. He had made an alliance with the enemy through marriage, and his wife, the infamous Jezebel, couldn't tolerate any true prophet of God. She attempted to kill all of the prophets of the LORD and impose Baal worship on all of Israel.

Baal worship was more serious than the golden calves already in their midst. The ten tribes of Israel (known as the northern kingdom) sinned away their day of grace and were eventually overcome and carried away into captivity by their enemies until their natural and spiritual identity was lost. This is very similar to what has happened to many nations and empires throughout history. America beware!

Even as the nation headed toward destruction, God worked through the prophets to redeem individuals attempting to turn the tide.

### Benhadad, the Enemy King, Attacked Ahab

*² And he sent messengers to Ahab, king of Israel, into the city and said unto him, Thus hath Benhadad said,*

*³ Thy silver and thy gold is mine; thy wives also and thy children, even the goodliest, are mine.*

*⁴ And the king of Israel answered and said, My lord, O king, according to thy word, I am thine and all that I have.*

*⁵ And the messengers came again and said, Thus hath Benhadad said, Although I have sent unto thee, saying, Thou shalt deliver me thy silver and thy gold and they wives and thy children,*

*⁶ yet I will send my slaves unto thee tomorrow about this time, and they shall search thy house and the houses of thy slaves; and it shall be that whatever is precious in thine eyes, they shall put it in their hand and take it away.*

*⁷ Then the king of Israel called all the elders of the land and said, Understand, I pray you, and see how this man seeks only evil, for he sent unto me for my wives and for my children and for my silver and for my gold, and I denied him not.*

*⁸ And all the elders and all the people said unto him, Hearken not unto him, nor consent.*

What did Ahab and his servants have in their houses that they didn't want to lose? Ahab was willing to give up his wives and his children, his silver and his gold, but he didn't want to let his enemy search his house, and he wasn't the only one. The elders and the people didn't want their houses searched either. What could have been more important to them than wives, children, silver, and gold? It was their idols.

We find an example of this that goes back to when Jacob (later Israel) left the land of his father-in-law, Laban, abruptly with his wives, children, and livestock. Before they left, his wife Rachel stole her father's household idols. In this account, we see the idols were more important to Laban than anything else, including his children and grandchildren (Genesis 31:17-35).

What idols do we have? In many churches today, the worship is a mixture of the things of God and the things of the world. This is very similar to Samaria. The names and forms of idols may change, but the evil spiritual forces behind them remain the same. So regardless of what our modern idols are called, rest assured the same demons are behind them. We can also be sure the idols are being used to control people and keep them separated from God. In God's eyes, this is an abomination, and he will eventually withdraw his presence and protection unless genuine repentance occurs.

> [9] So he said unto the messengers of Benhadad, Tell my lord the king, All that thou didst send for to thy slave at the first I will do, but this thing I may not do. And the messengers departed and brought him word again.
>
> [10] And Benhadad sent unto him again and said, The gods do so unto me, and more also, that the dust of Samaria shall not be enough for the open hands of all the people that follow me.
>
> [11] And the king of Israel answered and said, Tell him, Let not him that girds on his harness boast as he that puts it off.
>
> [12] And when he heard this word, as he was drinking with the kings in the pavilions, he said unto his slaves,

> Set yourselves in array. And they set themselves in array against the city.
>
> 13 And, behold, there came a prophet unto Ahab, king of Israel, saying, Thus hath the LORD said, Hast thou seen all this great multitude? Behold, I will deliver it into thy hand today, that thou shalt know that I am the LORD.

Who was this unnamed prophet? His style of ministry seems very similar to that which is later identified with Elisha. This wasn't a repent-or-else message. God's people, in their confused and contaminated state, were completely surrounded by a vastly superior enemy, and God decided to send his prophet with a message of deliverance and victory!

This same type of thing happened repeatedly during the deterioration of the Roman Empire, and it also happened during the decline of the British Empire. It seems to be happening now with the dwindling of American power. There is, however, a limit.

> 14 And Ahab said, By whom? And he said, Thus hath the LORD said, Even by the young men of the princes of the provinces. Then he said, Who shall begin the battle? And he answered, Thou.
>
> 15 Then he numbered the young men of the princes of the provinces, and they were two hundred and thirty-two: and after them he numbered all the people, even all the sons of Israel, being seven thousand.

Inside the walled fortress city of Samaria lived hundreds of thousands of people. Only seven thousand came out of the city to fight the enemy. Could these be the seven thousand mentioned in the previous chapter? God promised Elijah that he would cause seven thousand to remain in Israel (all the knees which hadn't bowed unto Baal and every mouth which hadn't kissed him).

> 16 And they went out at noon. But Benhadad was drinking himself drunk in the pavilions, he and the kings, the thirty-two kings that helped him.

> ¹⁷ And the young men of the princes of the provinces went out first. And Benhadad had sent out men who warned him, saying, There are men come out of Samaria.
>
> ¹⁸ Then he said, If they have come out for peace, take them alive; or if they have come out for war, take them alive.

Benhadad was drunk, and to him seven thousand men didn't seem to be much of a threat to his vast forces.

We are at a time in modern history when many leaders of the people of God are in a similar situation to Ahab. Even with seemingly good intentions, they are still married to a religious system as perverted as Jezebel. And believe it or not, we have come full circle in history, until once again the "king" of Syria and his friends, allies, and enemies are all major players upon the world stage. The natural battle lines are very similar to where they were in the book of Kings; the spiritual battle lines regarding the infiltration of the enemy inside the camp of the people of God are almost exactly the same.

Seeing the compromised and contaminated situation of some of the people of God today, one might think there isn't much of a possibility that God will back them up with his support. The forces of the corrupt world around us are against the people of God and making great advances on all sides. But nothing goes unnoticed by God. He overhears our enemies when they speak evil against him and use his name as if it were nothing. It doesn't go unnoticed when they blaspheme and declare themselves in agreement with the abominations taking place everywhere.

This is similar to some of the latest declarations made by certain national leaders. We will see what will happen. God could decide to take a hand in these matters, even when many of his people, along with many in our nation, don't deserve his interventions.

In King Ahab's case, God intervened twice in a row, defeating the enemy when Israel didn't really deserve victories. Even so, Ahab didn't change course. However, remember a remnant of humble people in the kingdom made up the seven thousand who never bowed their knees to Baal. Maybe God brought the victories for them, because in the kingdom of God, the least is really the greatest in God's eyes.

Some of us may think we are nothing, that we are insignificant and don't deserve to have God act in our favor. Truthfully, none of us "deserves" God's favor, but if our hearts are clean and we haven't bowed our knees before the god of this world, God can surprise us. Even if only a very small remnant is left, God can give the victory. Sodom could have been saved if only ten righteous men were found there, but sadly there was only one. In the days of Jeremiah, God would have spared Jerusalem for one righteous man, and there were none.

> [19] So these young men of the princes of the provinces came out of the city, and the army followed after them.
>
> [20] And each one smote the man that came against him; and the Syrians fled; and Israel pursued them. And Benhadad, the king of Syria, escaped on a horse with some of the horsemen.
>
> [21] And the king of Israel went out and smote the horsemen and the chariots and smote the Syrians with a great slaughter.
>
> [22] And the prophet came to the king of Israel and said unto him, Go strengthen thyself, and consider, and see what thou must do, for at the return of the year the king of Syria will come up against thee.

God hoped King Ahab and Israel would turn completely away from their idols, turn to him, and recognize that only he could keep them safe.

> [23] And the slaves of the king of Syria said unto him, Their gods are gods of the mountains; therefore, they were stronger than we; but let us fight against them in the plain, and surely we shall be stronger than they.
>
> [24] Therefore do this: Remove the kings from their positions and put captains in their place.
>
> [25] And prepare another army like the army thou hast lost, horse for horse and chariot for chariot; then we will fight

against them in the plain, and surely we shall be stronger than they. And he hearkened unto their voice and did so.

²⁶ And it came to pass at the return of the year, that Benhadad numbered the Syrians and went up to Aphek, to fight against Israel.

²⁷ And the sons of Israel were numbered and took provisions and went against them; and the sons of Israel pitched before them like two little flocks of kids; but the Syrians filled the land.

²⁸ Then the man of God came and spoke unto the king of Israel and said, Thus hath the LORD said, Because the Syrians have said, The LORD is God of the mountains, but he is not God of the valleys, therefore, I will deliver all this great multitude into thy hand that ye may know that I am the LORD.

²⁹ And they pitched one over against the other seven days. And so it was that in the seventh day the battle was joined; and the sons of Israel slew of the Syrians one hundred thousand footmen in one day.

Where are we today in recorded human history? We are at the end of six thousand years with the world in the hands of the devil. We are now entering the seventh millennium, which is the seventh prophetic day. Remember that one thousand years are as a day for the Lord (Psalm 90:4; 2 Peter 3:8). We are entering a time when there will be definitive battles (in both the spiritual and natural realms) regarding the future of the people of God and the future of the system of this world.

³⁰ But the rest fled to Aphec into the city, and the wall fell upon twenty-seven thousand of the men that were left. And Benhadad also fled and came into the city, into an inner chamber.

³¹ Then his slaves said unto him, Behold now we have heard that the kings of the house of Israel are merciful kings; let us, I pray thee, put sackcloth on our loins and

ropes upon our heads and go out to the king of Israel; peradventure he will give thee thy life.

What is the battle really about? This fight is with the devil, but it is also between the old carnal man and the new man in Christ. The fight that we are in now isn't with horses and chariots and swords. It is a fight for hearts, for souls. This is a fight where God doesn't desire for us to pardon certain enemies — such as the old man in Adam. If the old man with his old nature isn't put to death by the Spirit of God in each and every one of us, we won't be able to enter into our inheritance in Christ. The inheritance in Christ isn't for the old man; it is only for the new man. Therefore, with this in mind, look at the huge mistake Ahab made after God helped him to overcome his enemy.

> [32] So they girded sackcloth on their loins and put ropes on their heads and came to the king of Israel and said, Thy slave Benhadad saith, I pray thee, let me live. And he replied, If he is yet alive, he is my brother.
>
> [33] Now these men took this as a good omen and quickly took this word from his mouth, and they said, Thy brother Benhadad! And he said, Go ye, bring him. Then Benhadad came forth to him, and he caused him to come up into the chariot.

They believed in omens and it appears that King Ahab did too!

In the world and in much of the church, those who feel burdened by sin, when confronted with the reality of their sin, accept that they did wrong. They are willing to renounce the symptoms of their problem (adultery, thievery, etc.), but some never allow a deathblow to the root.

> [34] And Benhadad said unto him, The cities, which my father took from thy father, I will restore; and thou shalt make plazas for thee in Damascus, as my father made in Samaria, and I will leave here confederated with thee. So he made a covenant with him and sent him away.

In the Law of God, the kings of Israel are admonished not to trust in horses or in chariots. But Ahab had magnificent chariots; he had religious, political, and economic machinery powered by the flesh (the natural man), and he wasn't afraid to make an alliance with his enemy and to even invite him up into his chariot.

As Samaria had paid tribute to Damascus, now Damascus would pay tribute to Samaria. Benhadad means "son of power," and Benhadad was now offering to share his evil power with Ahab, the most evil king in the history of Israel!

Here is where the problem lies. Even when God gave Ahab the victory, Ahab preferred to make an alliance with the enemy rather than obey God. Throughout history, when God placed victory into the hands of leaders of the people of God, most weren't able to desist from the practices God advised them not to partake in. Instead, like Ahab, they preferred to unite themselves with the enemy rather than *completely* obey God. King Saul provides an example of a similar mistake with Agag the king of Amalek (1 Samuel 15:9).

> 35 Then a certain man of the sons of the prophets said unto his neighbor by the word of the LORD, Smite me, I pray thee. And the man refused to smite him.
>
> 36 The said he unto him, Because thou hast not obeyed the voice of the LORD, behold, as soon as thou art departed from me, a lion shall smite thee. And as soon as he was departed from him, a lion found him and smote him.
>
> 37 Then he found another man and said, Smite me, I pray thee. And the man smote him and wounded him.
>
> 38 So the prophet departed and waited for the king by the way and disguised himself with a veil over his eyes.
>
> 39 And as the king passed by, he cried unto the king, and he said, Thy slave went out into the midst of the battle; and behold, a man turned aside and brought a man unto me and said, Guard this man; if by any means he should get away, then shall thy life be for his life, or else thou shalt pay a talent of silver.

> ⁴⁰ And when thy slave was busy here and there, he disappeared. Then the king of Israel said unto him, So shall thy sentence be; thou thyself hast decided it.
> ⁴¹ Then he quickly took the veil away from his face; and the king of Israel recognized that he was of the prophets.
> ⁴² And he said unto him, Thus hath the LORD said, Because thou hast let go out of thy hand the man of my anathema, therefore, thy life shall go for his life and thy people for his people.
> ⁴³ And the king of Israel went to his house, sad and angry, and came to Samaria.

When Ahab received the victory from God over his immediate enemies, he made a fundamental mistake. He thought God's supernatural deliverance was a sign of God's approval upon him and upon his administration. This type of perception remains a huge problem today.

God, in his mercy, has shown much favor and delivered many people who haven't understood the true reasons behind what he has done. The misunderstanding lies in the fact that they perceive the miracle, blessing, or deliverance they experience as a sign of God's approval of them and their lifestyle, even though they are clearly operating in the fallen nature of Adam. They don't see that God is going to extreme lengths to demonstrate his love and character or that he deserves their utmost respect and devotion.

Ahab entirely missed the lesson God had for him. In addition to sparing Benhadad (symbol of the old man and old nature under the control of the devil), instead of repenting and returning to God, Ahab joined himself with Benhadad (who was anathema to God) by making a covenant with him.

When the old man, the old nature, is caught in a corner, he is capable of some extremely convincing negotiations. Benhadad put on sackcloth and plead for his life, and Ahab felt magnanimous by inviting him into his chariot and dealing with him. However, he didn't realize that letting his enemy go would eventually cost him his own life and the freedom of his people. If the old man continues to live in us, the Lord Jesus Christ cannot reign in and through us. It is that simple. If we continue to allow the old man to live, we will never be able to enter into the inheritance that God has for us.

We may live through victories along the way; we may have supernatural experiences; God may deliver us with his powerful hand, as he did with the children of Israel when he took them out of Egypt. When God delivered Israel out of Egypt, he demonstrated his power and sustained his people miraculously in the desert. But that generation didn't believe and obey God, and as a result all died in the wilderness with the exception of two men (Joshua and Caleb). Two out of millions entered into the Promised Land. The true inheritance of the fullness of the life of Christ cannot be shared with the old man.

The story of Ahab goes from bad to worse in the midst of tremendous grace and mercy from God upon the most evil king in the history of Israel. God continued to deliver his message through prophetic ministry in an all-out attempt to bring Ahab to repentance. This is a true indication of the heart of God, for he isn't willing that any should perish. But Ahab did not repent. He didn't *receive* the truth. Instead, he chose to take advice from his wife, and it proved to be fatal. Adam did something very similar.

We are living in a time when many are deceived, because they aren't willing to receive the truth. The only way for us to be saved from the deception is to embrace the Lord Jesus Christ in such a manner that the man of sin, the natural man, the old man, will have no place to hide.

If we persist and live in the presence of God, the presence of God will kill the man of sin. Each one of us is a battleground for this war. Outward appearances can be very deceptive. This is how Ahab, by God's grace, repeatedly won a battle but then lost the war.

One of my friends was the leader of a great Christian organization. He spent a lot of time, money, and effort building a secure headquarters. He put an armed guard at the entrance, video security surveillance around the grounds, and every employee wore an electronic badge that allowed them access to their specific area. His organization was prepared for a terrorist strike or an attack from a deranged gunman. But that isn't the type of attack that brought my friend down. The real enemy attack was entirely different. The devil used a very subtle internal attack by the old carnal nature to defeat my friend with devastating effectiveness.

But this is nothing compared to what is going on with the entire nation of the United States, which is paranoid about security and defense, as extreme security measures are being taken at airports, the borders, and even at courthouses and government installations.

Please don't misunderstand me. I'm not against taking reasonable security precautions. I would, however, point out that we've already been invaded. The demons are already inside our nation (even inside many of our churches), and they have almost complete control. Paranoia regarding our external security will never be able to truly defend us from our most dangerous threat. The spirit of this world is already in control of most of our universities and schools. It already controls most of Washington DC.

Jesus mused, *When the son of man comes, shall he find faith on the earth?* (Luke 18:8).

The earth is still under the curse, and while under the curse, it is impossible to produce good fruit. The only place possible to find good fruit (like faith) is where no curse is present. The only place, right now, where no curse exists is in the life of Christ. This is the real story of Elijah and Elisha.

Will Jesus find faith in us when he returns? He said we should know them by their fruit. Only the life of Jesus Christ produces good fruit, and he desires to live inside of us and take complete control of our entire being.

The tragic story of Ahab proves once again that it isn't enough to have gifts, ministry, and leadership. The fruit of the Spirit is essential, and it isn't something that can be manufactured by man. We know the Lord Jesus has already won the war, and he desires to empower us by his Spirit to walk in his victory. This is the battle presently being fought.

> Unless the LORD builds the house, they labour in vain that build it; unless the LORD keeps the city, the watchmen watch in vain. (Psalm 127:1)

**Let us pray:**

Heavenly Father, we ask for clarity so we may leave our own desires and aspirations aside and willingly do your will no matter what the cost.

May we be willing to surrender the old man upon your altar and desist from any last minute negotiations to keep him alive.

We ask this in the name of our Lord Jesus Christ. Amen.

# Chapter Five
## Naboth's Vineyard

King Ahab was struggling. He had gone from bad to worse in spite of incredible manifestations of God's mercy and grace. Like many of us, he misinterpreted the reasons behind God's dealings with him, because he remained totally focused on himself. Things were coming to a head, and the real state of his heart was about to be revealed.

Ahab had married Jezebel. She continually warred against the prophets of God, even after the Lord sent Elijah to confront the prophets of Baal and after the prophets of Baal were destroyed. In the midst of the terrible apostasy in Israel, God supernaturally delivered the nation on two occasions because of a faithful remnant of seven thousand persons who hadn't bowed the knee to Baal.

After the second victory, when Ahab had the opportunity to kill the enemy king once and for all, he joined himself with the enemy. God wasn't pleased. This is a lesson for all of us, because in one way or another we are all involved in this war. Each of us has a certain autonomy or self-rule, which can be compared to kings in the sense that each of us is king over our own lives.

If we decide not to follow the Lord, we will be subject to the consequences of not following the Lord. If we decide to embrace the lies of the enemy, we will be deceived, and our situation will deteriorate.

The decisions each of us makes have an effect on the present and the future. Our decisions may affect our families and friends, and they may affect our enemies. They may even result in consequences that will affect generations into the future. For this reason, our decisions are extremely important.

The decisions of these kings of Israel are written in Scripture (along with their consequences) for our edification, so we can learn from their experience. *And it came to pass after these things …* (1 Kings 21:1).

What things?

After God miraculously delivered Israel twice while the nation was experiencing unprecedented prosperity and apostasy under the most evil king in their history, King Ahab joined himself and the nation of Israel with the enemy king.

## 1 Kings 21

> ¹ And it came to pass after these things that Naboth of Jezreel had a vineyard which was in Jezreel, next to the palace of Ahab, king of Samaria.

Jezreel means "the LORD plants" and Scripture now describes Ahab as king of Samaria (meaning guard or watch) instead of king of Israel (he who prevails with God). Ahab is now degraded to a simple steward or caretaker instead of a prince with God.

> ² And Ahab spoke unto Naboth, saying, Give me thy vineyard that I may have it for a garden of herbs because it is next to my house, and I will give thee for it a better vineyard than it; or if it seems good unto thee, I will give thee the worth of it in money.
>
> ³ And Naboth replied unto Ahab, The LORD keep me from giving thee the inheritance of my fathers.

Ahab didn't have the concept of "The LORD keep me" He did things according to his own impulse, and he wanted Naboth's vineyard. In Israel property was carefully passed down from father to son and was a symbol of the blessing of God upon each family. Each inheritance had been carefully passed on since the time of Joshua and the conquest of Canaan.

If any Israelite fell in to debt and had to mortgage their land, it could only be sold until the year of Jubilee, at which time all property returned to the original owner. Obviously, in the years of kings like Ahab, they weren't practicing the years of Jubilee (every fiftieth year), and omissions such as this were mounting against them before the LORD.

In Naboth's vineyard, which was his inheritance from the LORD, the vine is a symbol of the life of God. So, symbolically, this was Naboth's God-given means to cultivate the very life of God. Ahab, the carnal man, desired to take this for himself and turn it into a herb garden. At first glance, this may seem naïve, but in agriculture, three stages exist: first the leaf (herb), then the flower, and ultimately the fruit.

The natural, carnal man in his fallen state is like an animal (a beast). The only thing he can understand about God is the part having to do with the leaf (the blade or the herb). He is like an animal that eats grass and gets fat. The natural man attempts to take the things of God to fatten himself. He wants to use God to get more and more of the things of this world.

In the natural realm of the Jews under the law, if they were diligent, they prospered at the natural level. This is true even today. Jews who haven't accepted the Lord Jesus and don't understand the real significance of the flower and the fruit continue to prosper in the things of this world. This also happens regarding many who call themselves Christians, but are carnal.

God's goal isn't for us to fatten ourselves in the things of this world. Rather, it is to prosper us in the life of God. Therefore, at times it may be better to have less of this world, if this causes our search for the Lord to intensify. The person with poor health may prosper spiritually above and beyond the person who has perfect health and has never had a problem. Only God knows.

If we put God first at every level of our existence, things will not necessarily all work out perfectly for us in this world. We will have trials and tribulations, and God will use the problems to draw us closer to him and cleanse our hearts before him.

Once he purifies our hearts (it is impossible for him to do this without our full cooperation), he will be able to prosper us in everything, and it will go well with us. He knows our hearts though and whether or not we harbor even small blots belonging to the old nature. God also knows how we will handle prosperity in the things of this world and whether it will result in corruption or growth.

The vineyard was a test for Naboth and also for Ahab. Naboth means "fruits" and implies maturity. Here Ahab is attempting to undermine Naboth's fruitfulness. Those like Ahab, who are immature and full of envy, will confront and come against those who are approaching maturity in Christ. Those like Ahab may appear to be very gifted on the outside, but they have absolutely no scruples.

> ⁴ And Ahab came into his house, sad and angry, because of the word which Naboth of Jezreel had spoken to him, for he had said, I will not give thee the inheritance of my fathers. And he lay down upon his bed and turned away his face and would eat no bread.

Ahab was acting like a spoiled child even though he was king. The consequences of his selfishness and pride were about to affect the legacy of his entire dynasty along with the nation.

> ⁵ And Jezebel, his wife, came to him and said unto him, Why is thy spirit so sad that thou dost eat no bread?
> ⁶ And he said unto her, Because I spoke with Naboth of Jezreel and said unto him, Give me thy vineyard for money; or else, if it please thee, I will give thee another vineyard for it; and he answered, I will not give thee my vineyard.
> ⁷ And Jezebel, his wife, said unto him, Dost thou now govern the kingdom of Israel? Arise and eat bread and let thy heart be merry; I will give thee the vineyard of Naboth of Jezreel.
> ⁸ So she wrote letters in Ahab's name and sealed them with his seal and sent the letters unto the elders and to the nobles that were in his city dwelling with Naboth.

The responsibility for this fell directly upon Ahab, even though it appeared Jezebel was the culprit. Notice that the letters were sealed with Ahab's seal or signet ring. Therefore Ahab was responsible.

> ⁹ And she wrote in the letters, saying, Proclaim a fast and set Naboth at the head of the people

> ¹⁰ and set two men, sons of Belial, before him, to bear witness against him, saying, Thou didst blaspheme God and the king. And then carry him out and stone him that he may die.

Sons of Belial were sons of the devil (satanists), an openly recognized meaning of this term. Ahab, the king of Israel, of the people of God, authorized this abomination when the letters were sealed with his ring. Today, in some religious environments, they don't actually have to kill people like Naboth; rumors and character assassination suffice.

> ¹¹ And the men of his city, even the elders and the nobles who were the inhabitants in his city, did as Jezebel had sent unto them and as it was written in the letters which she had sent unto them.
>
> ¹² They proclaimed a fast and set Naboth at the head of the people.
>
> ¹³ Then the two men of Belial, came in and sat before him; and those men of Belial witnessed against Naboth, in the presence of the people, saying, Naboth blasphemed God and the king. Then they carried him forth out of the city, and stoned him with stones that he died.

Notice that Jezebel knew exactly who she could rely on, and all the principle people of the city and the elders went along with her. No one pushed back. All of them had sold out their consciences, and no one raised a voice of protest. (This is how many like Hitler and Stalin obtained power.) What happened next sums this up:

> ¹⁴ Then they sent to Jezebel, saying, Naboth has been stoned and is dead.
>
> ¹⁵ And it came to pass when Jezebel heard that Naboth had been stoned and was dead that she said to Ahab, Arise, take possession of the vineyard of Naboth of Jezreel which he refused to give thee for money, for Naboth is not alive, but dead.

What Jezebel did with Naboth is very similar to what they did with Jesus and the majority of the apostles. Scripture makes it clear that dire consequences will fall upon the entire nation when innocent blood is shed, until finally the land will vomit its inhabitants, and desolation will set in. I believe there is a direct correlation between assassination of character and the many empty church buildings strewn across Europe and America.

> [16] And it came to pass when Ahab heard that Naboth was dead, that Ahab rose up to go down to the vineyard of Naboth of Jezreel, to take possession of it.
>
> [17] Then the word of the LORD came to Elijah, the Tishbite, saying,
>
> [18] Arise, go down to meet Ahab, king of Israel, who is in Samaria; behold, he is in the vineyard of Naboth, where he is gone down to possess it.

God sent his prophet to confront Ahab. God is still in the business of confronting those who follow the path of Ahab (Revelation 2:20-23).

> [19] And thou shalt speak unto him, saying, Thus hath the LORD said, Hast thou murdered and also taken possession? And thou shalt speak unto him again, saying, Thus hath the LORD said, In the same place where dogs licked the blood of Naboth shall the dogs lick thy blood, even thine.
>
> [20] And Ahab said to Elijah, Hast thou found me, O my enemy? And he answered, I have found thee because thou hast sold thyself to work evil in the sight of the LORD.

This was a very decisive moment in the life of Ahab. Until this point, he had done things by carnal impulse and negligence. For convenience, he had reversed priorities, but now Scripture states: *Thou hast sold thyself to work evil in the sight of the LORD.*

Today, in Israel, in the church, and in America, how many have sold themselves to work evil in the sight of the LORD?

Instead of working around the edges and being useful idiots who unwittingly help the real enemy of Israel, the church, our nation, and our souls, how many have blatantly trapped an innocent person with the intention of tearing down their reputation, so they could take something that wasn't theirs?

How much of this has gone on? I know it happens on a regular basis out in the world, but the sad truth is that it has also been happening among those who claim to be the people of God. Hear the Word of the LORD:

> 21 Behold, I will bring evil upon thee and will burn away thy prosperity and will cut off from Ahab him that pisses against the wall and he that is kept and he that is left in Israel.

Here is yet another serious warning from God that he will completely cut off the line of the carnal, natural man (Genesis 6:5-7) because *the wickedness of man is very great in the earth and every imagination of the thoughts of his heart is only evil continually.* The entire race of Adam is under judgment. The only salvation is found in Jesus Christ. It is only by the power of the Holy Spirit that we may put to death the deeds of the flesh (Romans 8:13). God says that the soul that sins shall surely die.

> 22 And I will make thy house like the house of Jeroboam, the son of Nebat and like the house of Baasha, the son of Ahijah, for the provocation with which thou hast provoked me to anger and made Israel to sin.
>
> 23 And of Jezebel, The LORD has also spoken, saying, The dogs shall eat Jezebel by the rampart of Jezreel.
>
> 24 Him that dies of Ahab in the city, the dogs shall eat, and him that dies in the field, shall the fowls of the air eat.
>
> 25 (Truly there was none like unto Ahab, who sold himself to work wickedness in the sight of the LORD, because Jezebel his wife incited him.
>
> 26 He was very abominable, following idols, according to all the things that the Amorites did, whom the LORD cast out before the sons of Israel.)

> ²⁷ And it came to pass, when Ahab heard those words, that he rent his clothes, and put sackcloth upon his flesh and fasted and slept in sackcloth and went softly.
>
> ²⁸ Then the word of the LORD came to Elijah, the Tishbite, saying,
>
> ²⁹ Seest thou how Ahab has humbled himself before me? Because he has humbled himself before me, I will not bring the evil in his days, but in his son's days I will bring the evil upon his house.

God's heart is very sensitive. Even in the case of wicked King Ahab, God was so pleased when Ahab repented that he decided not to bring the evil upon the house of Ahab while Ahab was still alive. This also gave Ahab's sons more time to repent and, in the same way, their choices could influence the heart of God.

In this passage we also see God treating Elijah as a close friend. He isn't just giving Elijah orders at this point; he is sharing his thoughts, feelings, and plans with Elijah!

This offers hope for anyone who truly humbles himself before the LORD. No matter how depraved, no matter how much evil he has done, it is still possible to move the heart of God by entering into genuine repentance.

Those who continue to go against their conscience slowly but surely lose their discernment until their reasoning is upside down. Many in leadership today have lost all sense of moral direction because their moral compass is now inverted. This provides impetus and impulse for them to apply as much pressure as possible on others to sell their consciences, too.

Our conscience (our moral compass that points to the truth) is one of the most important things we have received from God. If we don't take good care of it, we will not end well. It is that simple.

Everyone, no matter what his or her origin or background, is born with a conscience. If we follow our conscience, it will lead us to truth and to God. The more we affirm the truth and reject the lie, the clearer everything will be until the Holy Spirit is free in our heart, cleansing our entire being.

**Let us pray:**

Lord, we thank you that we are still able to perceive light and to discern the truth. We ask that our conscience continue to be refined by your Holy Spirit until the Morning Star is shining bright in our hearts, until a new day of righteousness dawns upon us and upon all of humanity. Amen.

# Chapter Six
## The Defeat of King Ahab is the Tipping Point

### 1 Kings 22

¹ And they continued three years without war between Syria and Israel.

² And it came to pass in the third year, that Jehoshaphat, the king of Judah, came down to the king of Israel.

³ And the king of Israel said unto his slaves, Know ye that Ramoth in Gilead is ours, and we are late in not taking it out of the hand of the king of Syria?

⁴ And he said unto Jehoshaphat, Wilt thou go with me to battle to Ramothgilead? And Jehoshaphat said to the king of Israel, I am as thou art, my people as thy people, my horses as thy horses.

The two kings made an alliance to fight against Syria. This agreement obviously would break the alliance Ahab had previously made with Benhadad, the king of Syria.

In the times of the divided kingdom, the southern kingdom of Judah was closer to the Lord. They had the temple in Jerusalem; they had the Levitical priesthood and still somewhat kept the feasts of the Lord. The practices of paganism infected the northern kingdom of Israel and eventually led them so far off course that the ten tribes of Israel were lost and completely disappeared.

This was like having an alliance today between Catholics and Protestants to win the world. (This isn't far from today's reality!)

⁵ And Jehoshaphat said unto the king of Israel, Enquire, I pray thee, at the word of the LORD today.

⁶ Then the king of Israel gathered the prophets together, about four hundred men, and said unto them, Shall I go

against Ramothgilead to battle, or shall I forbear? And they said, Go up, for the Lord shall deliver it into the hand of the king.

When Jehoshaphat used the name of the LORD in verse 5, he used the sacred name, which, according to tradition, wasn't to be pronounced. It means "I AM" in Hebrew. But when the "prophets" replied to the king, they used the word *Adoni*, which means "Lord" — an ambiguous term that could refer to God or Baal. This switch in terminology wasn't lost on Jehoshaphat who threw that ball back into their court.

> 7 And Jehoshaphat said, Is there even yet a prophet of the LORD here that we might enquire of him?

Jehoshaphat used the sacred name of the LORD again and made it clear he wanted to hear from a real prophet of the LORD. Today the religious world is full of prophets whose word seems true, but doubt remains. Are they really prophets of the LORD?

> 8 And the king of Israel replied unto Jehoshaphat, There is yet one man, Micaiah, the son of Imlah, by whom we may enquire of the LORD; but I hate him, for he does not prophesy good concerning me, but evil. And Jehoshaphat said, Let not the king say so.
> 
> 9 Then the king of Israel called a eunuch and said, Bring Micaiah, the son of Imlah, here quickly.

Many passages in Scripture refer to only one true prophet and many false prophets. Scripture also states *the testimony of Jesus is the spirit of prophecy* (Revelation 19:10). The only trustworthy prophecy is one sent by Jesus through the Holy Spirit.

> 10 And the king of Israel and Jehoshaphat, the king of Judah, sat each on his throne, having put on their robes, in the plaza at the entrance of the gate of Samaria, and all the prophets prophesied before them.
> 
> 11 And Zedekiah, the son of Chenaanah, made himself horns of iron, and he said, Thus hath the LORD said,

With these shalt thou push the Syrians until thou have consumed them.

Iron is symbolic of the law. Many in both the secular and religious realm believe the law (or at least their laws) will give us victory over our enemies. That assumption couldn't be further from the truth.

<sup>12</sup> And all the prophets prophesied so, saying, Go up to Ramothgilead and be prospered, for the LORD shall deliver it into the king's hand.

<sup>13</sup> And the messenger that had gone to call Micaiah spoke unto him, saying, Behold now, the words of the prophets declare good unto the king with one mouth; now let thy word, I pray thee, be like the word of one of them and speak that which is good.

The messenger thought that the messages delivered by all the other prophets were good. It never even dawned on him that the consequences would be serious if they were mistaken.

<sup>14</sup> And Micaiah said, As the LORD lives, all that the LORD says unto me, that will I speak.

<sup>15</sup> So he came to the king. And the king said unto him, Micaiah, shall we go against Ramothgilead to battle, or shall we forbear? And he answered him, Go and be prospered, for the LORD shall deliver it into the hand of the king.

<sup>16</sup> And the king said unto him, How many times shall I adjure thee that thou tell me nothing but that which is true in the name of the LORD?

<sup>17</sup> Then he said, I saw all Israel scattered upon the mountains as sheep without a shepherd; and the LORD said, These have no master; let them return each man to his house in peace.

<sup>18</sup> And the king of Israel said unto Jehoshaphat, Did I not tell thee that he would not prophesy good concerning me, but evil?

¹⁹ Then he said, Hear thou, therefore, the word of the LORD: I saw the LORD sitting on his throne and all the host of the heavens standing by him on his right hand and on his left.

²⁰ And the LORD said, Who shall persuade Ahab that he may go up and fall at Ramothgilead? And one said in this manner and another in that manner.

²¹ And there came forth a spirit and stood before the LORD and said, I will persuade him.

²² And the LORD said unto him, In what manner? And he said, I will go forth, and I will be a lying spirit in the mouth of all his prophets. And he said, Thou shalt persuade him, and prevail also, go forth and do so.

²³ Now, therefore, behold, the LORD has put a lying spirit in the mouth of all these thy prophets, and the LORD has decreed evil concerning thee.

²⁴ Then Zedekiah, the son of Chenaanah, went near and smote Micaiah on the cheek and said, Which way did the Spirit of the LORD go from me to speak unto thee?

²⁵ And Micaiah said, Behold, thou shalt see in that day when thou shalt go into an inner chamber to hide thyself.

²⁶ Then the king of Israel said, Take Micaiah and carry him back unto Amon, the governor of the city and to Joash, the king's son

²⁷ and say, Thus hath the king said, Put this fellow in the prison and feed him with bread of affliction and with water of affliction, until I return in peace.

²⁸ And Micaiah said, If thou return at all in peace, the LORD has not spoken by me. Then he said, Hearken, O people, every one of you.

The New Testament speaks of the deception of iniquity working in those who perish, because they didn't receive the love of the truth to be saved (2 Thessalonians 2:10).

In the Old Testament, King Saul received an evil spirit sent from the LORD when he rejected the truth (1 Samuel 16:14-15).

The book of Job describes a similar scene in heaven *when the sons of God came to present themselves before the LORD and Satan came also among them* (Job 1:6). Even in his fallen state, Satan must respect the limits God placed on him. He was allowed to afflict Job in many ways, but God told Satan that he couldn't take Job's life (Job 2:6).

It is clear that the lying spirit God put in the mouth of the prophets of Ahab wasn't the Holy Spirit, because the Holy Spirit is the Spirit of Truth.

> 29 So the king of Israel and Jehoshaphat, the king of Judah, went up to Ramothgilead.

Modern historians aren't sure of the exact location of Ramothgilead. It is believed to be near where Syria, Jordan, and the Golan Heights all come together. It was undoubtedly a strategic location outside of the present borders of Israel.

Both kings obviously thought it so desirable for the security and prosperity of their kingdoms that they were willing to start a major war with Syria. Spiritually, Ramothgilead represents the high ground, which is lost and presently out of the reach of the church. Large sectors of Christians (Catholic, Protestant, or Orthodox) don't seem to believe it is really possible to live in victory. Over the centuries, they have relinquished the spiritual high ground to the enemy, yet they continue to dream about retaking what they perceive they have lost in both the natural and spiritual realms. However, it is impossible to regain this type of ground from the enemy without being clean and without being under the direct orders of the LORD.

> 30 And the king of Israel said unto Jehoshaphat, I will disguise myself and enter into the battle, but put thou on thy robes. And the king of Israel disguised himself and went into the battle.

The king of Israel knew that Benhadad, the king of Syria, would be furious with him for breaking the covenant the two of them had made three years before. So he disguised himself before going into battle, while he encouraged the king of Judah to dress in his royal robes. Ahab figured that the enemy would go after Jehoshaphat instead of him, because Jehoshaphat would be clearly recognizable as a king.

> ³¹ But the king of Syria commanded his thirty-two captains that had rule over his chariots, saying, Fight neither with small nor great, but only with the king of Israel.
> ³² And when the captains of the chariots saw Jehoshaphat, they said, Surely this is the king of Israel. And they turned aside to fight against him, but Jehoshaphat cried out.

Jehoshaphat, meaning "whom the LORD judges," realized he'd been set up by Ahab and cried out. Here is a parallel passage:

> And when the captains of the chariots saw Jehoshaphat, they said, It is the king of Israel. Therefore, they compassed about him to fight; but Jehoshaphat cried out, and the LORD helped him; and God separated them from him. (2 Chronicles 18:31)

And here we pick up the account in 1 Kings 22.

> ³³ And it came to pass, when the captains of the chariots perceived that it was not the king of Israel, that they turned back from pursuing him.
> ³⁴ But a certain man, shooting his bow in perfection, smote the king of Israel between the joints of his coat of mail; therefore, he said unto the driver of his chariot, Turn thy hand and carry me out of the host, for I am wounded.
> ³⁵ And the battle had increased that day, and the king was stayed up in his chariot against the Syrians and died in the evening, and the blood ran out of the wound into the midst of the chariot.
> ³⁶ And at the going down of the sun there went a proclamation throughout the camp, saying Every man to his city and every man to his own land.
> ³⁷ So the king died and was brought to Samaria, and they buried the king in Samaria.

> ³⁸ And they washed the chariot in the pool of Samaria, and they also washed his armour; and the dogs licked up his blood, according unto the word of the LORD which he had spoken.

The Hebrew word translated here as *armour* can also mean *fornications*. I'll go into more detail later.

> ³⁹ Now the rest of the acts of Ahab and all that he did, and the ivory house which he made and all the cities that he built, are they not written in the book of the chronicles of the kings of Israel?
> ⁴⁰ So Ahab slept with his fathers, and Ahaziah, his son, reigned in his stead.

This was the end of the infamous King Ahab, the most evil king in the history of Israel. Even so, God granted him more time when he humbled himself before the Lord. It wasn't, however, a complete repentance. For this reason, he didn't have enough discernment to recognize the warning from God that came through the only true prophet rather than listen to the contaminated prophets who had a lying spirit sent from the LORD.

In Hebrew, the word for *royal robes* and the word for a seamless suit of chain mail or body armor that protected the kings of Israel from the neck down is the same. When Ahab decided to disguise himself, it meant that he used the standard armor issued for a typical chariot commander. This consisted of a breastplate and back plate joined at the sides by a leather harness. This is where the arrow penetrated his armor. Ironically, the word for the *common armor* he used and the word for *fornications* is the same word.

Spiritually this equates to disguising himself in a way that sent him into battle without a breastplate of righteousness or weapons of faith and truth. Instead his weapons were described as "fornications" due to his unclean state. Later on, in the history of Judah, King Josiah came to a similar fate (2 Chronicles 35:20-24).

On the other hand, God defended righteous King Jehoshaphat as he went into battle wearing his royal armor, which attracted the attention of the enemy captains.

Question: Today we have people who consider themselves to be kings over the people of God, yet who aren't clean. What if they do things their own way as they consolidate power, and their churches are full of prophets who prophesy that they will unite the people of God all over the world and win a great victory in the name of the Lord over the forces of evil? How can they know if a lying spirit is in the mouths of all their prophets?

What we do know is that one true prophetic voice from outside their circle of influence is saying, "All of this is going to come to a bad end." They have cast out the true prophets and have them on a diet of bread and water of affliction.

Every day we are getting closer to the decisive battle. The enemy will attack and they won't just attack anyone. The enemy will attack those whom God specifies.

Isn't this intriguing?

Those misrepresenting the Lord, enslaving the people of God, and doing things in God's name without considering whether they are doing things pleasing to him, will seek results they desire, armed with weapons other than weapons of the Lord. These will all be defeated in the battle.

As we head into battle, we shouldn't use the tactics our enemies use. They may use schemes like calling people to orchestrate their own plans, saying things like, "Don't go to such and such a meeting," or "Don't support this or that person." And yet, when you encounter these same people face-to-face, they'll smile a hypocritical smile and speak to you in a friendly manner, while they continue to make subversive phone calls behind your back.

This type of behavior may continue for a time, but it won't continue forever. Things will go one way or the other. In Judah, the trajectory of King Jehoshaphat went mostly in the right direction, even in the face of many obstacles (one of which was Ahab).

> 41 And Jehoshaphat, the son of Asa, began to reign over Judah in the fourth year of Ahab, king of Israel.
>
> 42 Jehoshaphat was thirty-five years old when he began to reign, and he reigned twenty-five years in Jerusalem. His mother's name was Azubah, the daughter of Shilhi.

> ⁴³ And he walked in all the ways of Asa, his father; he turned not aside from it, doing that which was right in the eyes of the LORD. Nevertheless, the high places were not taken away, for the people offered and burnt incense yet in the high places.
>
> ⁴⁴ And Jehoshaphat made peace with the king of Israel.

Jehoshaphat made peace with Ahab by marrying Ahab's daughter. This was a major mistake by an otherwise exemplary king. Asa, his godly father, had also shown a lapse in judgment when he hired Benhadad, king of Syria, with money from the LORD's treasury to fight Baasha king of Israel. Instead of relying on the LORD, he fought a king who was causing him a lot of trouble with this tactic.

Jehoshaphat may have been trying to compensate for his father's costly error when he made the unholy alliance with Ahab, just as Ahab was about to break his unholy covenant with Benhadad. However, God looks at the heart and doesn't destroy the righteous along with the wicked.

In my own personal experience, I have also found that God doesn't allow those who are righteous to be destroyed even if they make honest mistakes. Such blunders can still be very painful to go through though—a lesson Jehoshaphat learned the hard way. He was almost killed when the enemy captains mistook him for Ahab, because Ahab had purposely disguised himself while leaving Jehoshaphat exposed. In the midst of his problem, Jehoshaphat cried out to the LORD and the LORD delivered him.

> ⁴⁵ Now the rest of the acts of Jehoshaphat and his might that he showed and how he warred, are they not written in the book of the chronicles of the kings of Judah?

According to 2 Chronicles, Jehoshaphat had a magnificent army with hundreds of thousands of soldiers, so most of the nations around him feared to attack him.

> ⁴⁶ And the remnant of the male cult prostitutes, which had remained from the days of his father, Asa, he consumed out of the land.

⁴⁷ There was no king in Edom, there was a president instead of a king.

⁴⁸ Jehoshaphat had made ships in Tharshish to go to Ophir for gold, but they did not go, for the ships were broken at Eziongeber.

⁴⁹ Then Ahaziah, the son of Ahab, said unto Jehoshaphat, Let my slaves go with thy slaves in the ships but Jehoshaphat would not.

Calls and offers come across our paths, asking us to take part in opportunities for outreach or other activities. When they do, it is absolutely essential that we hear from the Lord regarding each case or situation, because many of the LORD's good people have gotten into trouble by joining with those who aren't clean.

Jehoshaphat survived a very close call. He did not listen to the only prophet of the LORD that Ahab could produce. He also witnessed Ahab sticking this true prophet, Micaiah, in jail for proclaiming the true Word of the LORD. Finally, he accompanied Ahab into battle against the counsel of the LORD and witnessed Ahab's tragic end.

Jehoshaphat learned his lesson from this experience, but further consequences of the unholy family alliance between Jehoshaphat and the family of Ahab later proved fatal to his son and caused untold damage to the nation of Judah.

⁵⁰ And Jehoshaphat slept with his fathers and was buried with his fathers in the city of David, his father, and Jehoram, his son, reigned in his stead.

⁵¹ Ahaziah, the son of Ahab, began to reign over Israel in Samaria in the year seventeen of Jehoshaphat, king of Judah, and reigned two years over Israel.

⁵² And he did evil in the sight of the LORD and walked in the way of his father and in the way of his mother and in the way of Jeroboam, the son of Nebat, who made Israel sin,

> ⁵³ for he served Baal and worshipped him and provoked to anger the LORD God of Israel, according to all that his father had done.

This concludes the book of 1 Kings. We have had many "kings" in the history of the church as well as many divisions, even though 1 Corinthians 1:10 tells us to have no divisions among us. Over the years many have come up with ideas for ways to reconcile and unite Christianity. But many of these plans God did not prosper, because they were Ahab-style attempts to unify Christians.

They failed because the armor of Ahab isn't the armor of God. Ahab's armor contained fornications, evil deeds, and the shedding of innocent blood. He even managed to make an alliance with righteous Jehoshaphat who ended up being very fortunate to escape with his life.

Leaders like Ahab can be found in the church and in Israel today, and the vast majority of their followers are unclean. As in so many biblical examples, a day of reckoning is looming upon our modern horizon. Evil grows worse and worse, but it will finally come to a head as the end-time battle is joined. There will also be an unprecedented display of the love, mercy, and power of God.

As we journey into the book of 2 Kings, we'll find that even in the midst of ever-increasing wickedness and perversion among the supposed the people of God, there is an important change in the ministry of the prophets. In 1 Kings the prophets struggled. In 2 Kings the prophets are victorious. The transition from one book to the next appears to be the tipping point. All of this is written in the Scriptures for our edification, and I believe it is a blueprint for the end times in which we now live.

**Let us pray:**

Heavenly Father, we ask for great wisdom, and in the difficult days ahead may we have discernment to embrace those who are clean, those who are yours. May we be willing to lay down our lives for the brethren. But let us also discern those who are corrupt, so we do not join forces with those who do not love cleanliness or join with those who are not using the right weapons.

Open our eyes that we may be able to identify those whose arms and armor are contaminated and help us distance ourselves from them.

We ask this in the name of our Lord Jesus Christ. Amen.

# Part II
# The New Day in God Is Dawning

# Chapter Seven
## Elijah Enters the Realm of Total Victory

### 2 Kings 1

¹ Then Moab rebelled against Israel after the death of Ahab.

Moab had been paying tribute to Israel, but at the time of Ahab's death, they decided to rebel. This is covered in 2 Kings 3.

² And Ahaziah fell down through a lattice in his upper chamber that was in Samaria and was sick, and he sent messengers and said unto them, Go, enquire of Baalzebub, the god of Ekron, whether I shall recover of this disease.

Ahaziah was the son of Ahab.

³ But the angel of the LORD said to Elijah, the Tishbite, Arise, go up to meet the messengers of the king of Samaria, and thou shalt say unto them, Is there no God in Israel, that ye go to enquire of Baalzebub, the god of Ekron?

⁴ Now therefore, thus hath the LORD said, Thou shalt not come down from that bed on which thou art gone up, but shalt surely die. And Elijah departed.

⁵ And when the messengers turned back unto him, he said unto them, Why are ye now turned back?

⁶ And they said unto him, We met a man who said unto us, Go, turn again unto the king that sent you and say unto him, Thus hath the LORD said, Is there no God in Israel, that thou dost send to enquire of Baalzebub, the god of Ekron? Therefore thou shalt not come down from that bed on which thou art gone up, but shalt surely die.

⁷ Then he said unto them, What manner of man was he who came up to meet you and told you these words?

⁸ And they answered him, He was a hairy man and girt with a girdle of leather about his loins. And he said, It is Elijah, the Tishbite.

Since the days when God covered Adam and Eve with coats of skin after their sin made them aware of their nakedness (Genesis 3:21), the leather girdle has been a symbol of a blood covenant between the person wearing the girdle and God. The blood covenant represents a change of life *for the life of the flesh is in the blood* (Leviticus 17:11). This is the meaning behind the temple rites and sacrifices involving blood.

The prophet Elijah wore this symbol because he lived as a clean vessel through which God could do his will. God spoke through him, so he could show the people the things of God.

Many among the people, like the kings of Israel, weren't in covenant with God. Instead of seeking God's will, they sought their own pleasure. As a result, it was much easier for them to consult the god of Ekron (who was a demon) than to consult the Lord of heaven. The LORD required that his peoples' lives be placed upon the altar of God in order for him to implement his will in or through them. Those who desired to live seeking the things of this world were always distant and aloof from the LORD.

All the nations sought the god of this world, but the people of Israel were to be different. They were the people of God. This is why God became angry with them. They acted like the world and continually sought other gods.

Ahab had a sentence upon him, not just because he'd sought to live his own life (as king of the people of God while refusing to listen to God), but also because he killed innocent Naboth who refused to give Ahab his God-given inheritance. God had sent Elijah to Ahab to tell him that God had dictated judgment upon Ahab and upon his posterity.

When Ahab repented, God changed his sentence and declared that the judgment against the house of Ahab would take place during his son's days (1 Kings 21:20-29). The sons of Ahab, however, instead of repenting, insisted on consulting demons instead of God.

When Elijah confronted the messengers of Ahab's son, Ahaziah, look what he did:

> ⁹ Then the king sent unto him a captain of fifty with his fifty. And he went up to him, and, behold, he sat on the top of a mountain. And he spoke unto him, Man of God, the king has commanded thee to come down.

The New Testament states that all of these Old Testament accounts were written for our benefit, so we won't repeat the same mistakes the children of Israel made (1 Corinthians 10:11-12). So what can we learn from this verse? First, it's significant to note that fifty is an important number in the Scriptures. It is the number of pentecost and the Feast of Pentecost, which was fulfilled in Acts 2 and represents the Christian Church.

This verse in 2 Kings isn't just about a strange event involving weird kings that took place almost three thousand years ago. It's an example for us today of what may happen in the Christian Church and modern Israel when men and women, who desire to reign over the people of God, do things their own way instead of God's way. It can result in worshipping devils.

This type of behavior hasn't only allowed demons access to their people, but like Ahab, when a real prophet of the Lord shows up, they act high-handed and downright nasty. For instance, consider the first captain in our example. This captain, with his fifty soldiers, was sent to bring Elijah in by force, and the captain had a definite attitude, saying, *Man of God, the king has commanded thee to come down!*

Elijah was on the top of a mountain, which symbolizes the presence of God.

> ¹⁰ And Elijah answered and said to the captain of fifty, If I am a man of God, then let fire come down from heaven, and consume thee and thy fifty. And fire came down from heaven, that consumed him and his fifty.

The king and his men had never been thwarted in such a manner! Ahab and his wife, Jezebel, were accustomed to doing whatever they pleased with the prophets of God (Matthew 5:10-12). Jezebel and her men had persecuted, banished, and murdered many prophets. Ahab, in the presence of godly King Jehoshaphat, had sentenced the true prophet Micaiah to prison with his only food being the bread and water of affliction.

In the church age, we also have experienced a long history in which true Christians, the true believers who are in a blood covenant with God (so the Lord can live his life in us) have been killed, persecuted, and banished by the sons of "Ahab" and "Jezebel" according to their every whim (Hebrews 11).

Pagan Rome is estimated to have killed about seven million Christians, many of whom were fed to lions in the Coliseum. Christian Rome is reported to have martyred over seventy million believers in the Spanish Inquisition alone. Christian Orthodox Constantinople also tortured, killed, and mutilated untold millions. Yet more Christians are being persecuted and killed today than ever before. Religious people tend to be much more fanatical about killing and persecuting the true prophets of God than those who aren't religious. The number fifty in Scripture describes religious people and the age of pentecost.

However, a most remarkable change took place between 1 Kings and 2 Kings. It has to do with God's true prophets and their ministry. Why weren't the forty-six chapters of Kings left as one book? Why divide these accounts into two books, and why break at this particular place?

The Lord desires to show us something important concerning a division in history — a time where the rules will change. This happens after the death of Ahab and before the death of Jezebel (Revelation 2:20-23). It is an example, which has its modern day counterpart.

A few days before this division of time, in the period symbolically covered in 1 Kings, if the king would have sent his fifty soldiers with their captain, they would most likely have laid hands on Elijah like they did with Micaiah a few days before. They had seized Micaiah (meaning who is like the LORD) and put him in jail on bread and water until the king returned from the battle, but the king never returned.

It was after Ahab failed to return that the rules changed. The son of Ahab thought he could do the same to Elijah, and the death of fifty soldiers didn't cause him to change his mind or hesitate to send another fifty. He couldn't believe a game changer had occurred.

When the first atomic bomb fell on Japan, they couldn't believe it either. It took the second atomic bomb for them to begin to understand the full magnitude of what had happened and that their only option was unconditional surrender. A new day dawned, and the rules of warfare had radically changed. Until this time, people were taught the atom couldn't be split, but now the unthinkable had happened. The age of nuclear power and weapons had arrived. This could take one of two basic forms. A controlled reaction could produce peaceful energy, or an uncontrolled chain reaction could create terrible new weapons of mass destruction.

Between the point where 1 Kings ends and 2 Kings begins, a change occurred in the way certain things happened. We are living at the very edge of a similar change regarding the spiritual realm. The day of man is at its end, and we stand at the beginning of what Scripture calls the day of the LORD. In some ways, this may be similar to events surrounding the first coming of Jesus Christ. From the birth of baby Jesus in the manger at Bethlehem to the total destruction of the temple and Jerusalem was about seventy years. During this time, the day or age of the law was closing and the age of grace (of the church) was opening. The next prophetic event on God's calendar is what Scripture in a total of thirty-two references describes as the day of the LORD.

Historians have divided history, thinking they know how and where to divide. For instance, many divide time before Christ and after Christ, thinking the first coming is the focal point of human history. And yes, it was a key change. When the Lord came the first time, many things changed. With his first coming, he brought the possibility of a new covenant as well as the placing of the earnest (or down payment) of the Spirit of God inside all believers (2 Corinthians 1:22; 5:5; Ephesians 1:13-14). But this won't be the final dividing point of history. The true division of human history is about to occur now, as the day of man ends and we enter into the real day of the LORD and the fullness of the Spirit is poured out (the fullness of our inheritance in Christ). The exact timing and many details regarding the second coming of the Lord Jesus Christ and the age to come are still shrouded in mystery until *the day of the voice of the seventh angel when he shall begin to sound the trumpet* (Revelation 10:7). Yet we know that the second coming will be preceded by key signs and changes that only the elect will recognize (Matthew 24; Mark 13; Luke 21).

The manner in which they have been able to do things against the true servants of God will change. At first, this change won't be obvious to many. Many despots who reign over, control, and demand things from the people of God won't believe it, just like Ahab's son didn't believe his power to do as he pleased to the true prophets had changed. And just like Ahab's son, Ahaziah, they will have serious problems. This is happening even now.

I don't know if you are aware of the news, but great "kings" in the Christian realm are no longer able to do things as they have always done them, because the light is beginning to uncover their practices. Many of these so-called Christian leaders find themselves in the same circumstance as King Ahaziah. They think they reign. They give extreme orders. But they are on their deathbed, and the Word of the LORD says "they shall not recover." Their realms are full of false prophets, and they insist on consulting those who are void of the Spirit of God. Their gifts and ministries will soon come to an end, as the new day of God dawns.

King Ahaziah was very slow to catch on to the new dimension of the prophetic ministry of Elijah.

## 2 Kings 1

> [11] *Again also he sent unto him another captain of fifty with his fifty. And he answered and said unto him, O man of God, thus hath the king said, Come down quickly.*

The first captain said, *The king has commanded thee to come down.* This second captain said, *The king said, Come down quickly.* Still very imposing; still showed no respect for Elijah. They thought that he had no "covering," no respect for their authority, and he was a lone ranger who didn't submit to anyone. They considered those like Elijah to be loose cannons.

> ¹² And Elijah answered and said unto them, If I am a man of God, let fire come down from heaven and consume thee and thy fifty. And the fire of God came down from heaven and consumed him and his fifty.

*If I am a man of God* … The Hebrew word translated *man* denotes a freeborn man (not a slave). The king thought everyone was his slave, but even his servants were calling Elijah a free man.

Therefore, Elijah answered, *"If I am a (freeborn) man of God …?* Then why are you here with fifty soldiers to lay hands on me and take me before the king?"

This was the third time the fire of God fell from heaven in the ministry of Elijah: Once before when he faced the prophets of Baal, and now twice to show the king and his army that they no longer had authority over a true prophet of God.

The name Elijah can mean "God Himself." The Lord's true prophetic ministry happens where God himself operates. When he implements a true blood covenant, it means we are to be dead and God alive in us by the Holy Spirit. When this happens, it is God himself. The king, however, didn't give up.

> ¹³ And he sent again a captain of the third fifty with his fifty. And the third captain of fifty went up and came and fell on his knees before Elijah and besought him and said unto him, O man of God, I pray thee, let my life and the life of these fifty thy slaves, be precious in thy sight.
>
> ¹⁴ Behold, fire has come down from heaven and burnt up the two captains of the former fifties with their fifties; therefore, let my soul now be precious in thy sight.

The third captain came with a changed attitude — a big change. He didn't impose. He realized the reality of this precise time in history and that the life of Elijah wasn't at his mercy. The captain of the army and his fifty men were now at the mercy of Elijah and of what he would say in the name of the Lord. The third captain understood this situation perfectly. He dropped humbly on his knees and pleaded for his life and the lives of his men. His actions show how roles had changed. He and his men were now the slaves. Slaves of whom? Of God himself, of Elijah. Isn't this a great accomplishment?

Brethren, we are entering a new day, a different day, a day in which the lukewarm are now in grave danger; but those in a blood covenant with God, in whom God is alive, are secure in the life of God.

The *kings* who have lorded it over God's people have propagated lies and deception saying, "Things will get worse and worse for God's people, until just before the devil takes over everything, and then God will rapture his church. Believers will all mysteriously disappear to heaven, and the devil will consolidate his kingdom and reign here on earth for three and a half, or seven, or even seventy years."

Nothing could be further from the truth. The devil has reigned here on earth for the past six thousand years. He hasn't consolidated his kingdom, because the very nature of his kingdom won't permit it. The devil's kingdom will never be united, because his followers always fight with one another.

None of the biblical patterns and end-time descriptions prophesy a unified, one world government in the hands of the devil. As time advances, corruption grows worse, and rather than unity, things become more and more fragmented. More kings, more heads, more division. The monster of Revelation doesn't have one head. It has seven heads, which in biblical prophetic language means the complete number of heads.

The statue in the book of Daniel, which symbolizes the kingdoms that will dominate the world, doesn't end united. It crumbles to ten fragmented toes made of baked clay and iron that refuse to mix (like modern democracies and the rule of law), as a stone cut without hands crashes into the feet of the image and turns it all into dust which is scattered by the wind.

Daniel declared that *the wicked shall get worse; and none of the wicked shall understand*. And that: *those that understand shall shine as the brightness of the firmament* (Daniel 12:10, 3).

God won't take his people away and hide them. No, he will put them on display. Elijah was sitting on the top of a mountain where everyone could see him. This confrontation took place in the sight of everyone (Matthew 5:14). After this, the prophets were able to dwell and prosper openly throughout Israel, and there is no evidence that Jezebel was able to hurt them, even though everything else in Israel was seemingly unchanged.

At the proper time, God will give the kingdom to the saints, and his kingdom will never be corrupted or taken over by those who are unclean (Daniel 7:13-14). The time has come, and is even at the door, when, like Elijah, those whom God chooses will be able to stand firm before any situation, and no one will be able to remove them. This will mark a major transition between the age of grace and the age of the kingdom. In Scripture one prophetic picture of this happens right between the end of 1 Kings and the beginning of 2 Kings.

When the third captain came to Elijah, he began to realize a substantial change had taken place. The king (on his deathbed) no longer had any jurisdiction over the prophets of God.

> ¹⁵ Then the angel of the LORD said unto Elijah, Go down with him; do not be afraid of him. And he arose and went down with him unto the king.

But notice the message to the king isn't saying, "Look King! Do you realize what just happened up on that mountain? So far this has cost you one hundred soldiers and two captains, but you may have one last chance."

No! The king had already sinned away his day of grace.

> ¹⁶ And he said unto him, Thus hath the LORD said, Forasmuch as thou hast sent messengers to enquire of Baalzebub, the god of Ekron, peradventure is there no God in Israel to enquire of his word? Therefore, thou shalt not

come down off that bed on which thou art gone up, but
shalt surely die.

Ahaziah means "the LORD has seized." In the year of liberty, the LORD will seize the gifts and ministries given to slaves, and only the true sons who submitted to his discipline and correction will receive the inheritance (Ezekiel 46:17).

> ¹⁷ So he died according to the word of the LORD which
> Elijah had spoken. And Jehoram (son of Ahab) reigned
> in his stead, in the second year of Jehoram, the son of
> Jehoshaphat, king of Judah because Ahaziah had no son.

The house of Ahab, in the life of Adam, cannot produce sons of God (joint heirs with Christ). It only produces slaves to sin, the world, and the devil.

> ¹⁸ Now the rest of the acts of Ahaziah which he did, are
> they not written in the book of the chronicles of the kings
> of Israel?

Note that Elijah wrote a scathing letter to Jehoram, the son of Jehoshaphat, mentioned in 2 Chronicles 21:12.

As this line of the prophetic ministry of Elijah continues in the book of 2 Kings into the double portion of Elisha and beyond, God's prophets are never forced to run from any situation. They are able to come forward with the Word of the LORD and stand firm. It is their enemies who have to run.

All of this happened in the midst of a world where corruption continually increased among the ten tribes of Israel until they were completely destroyed and consumed. Our present world situation will also come to a bad end. However, God's remnant, who represent him the way he desires, will be present, and many souls will be won for the kingdom of God, even as the kingdoms of men fail.

The Lord is about to do something, beginning with the corrupt *kings* reigning over the people of God. They are about to collide with reality and won't recover from their present deathbed.

The god of this world, the devil, is also about to receive a mortal blow. The entire system of this world, including the religious system, will receive a blow from which it won't recover. This won't take place because we planned it. The blow will fall when the LORD decides. This will be from a stone cut without hands, without our intervention. The most we can do is announce, warn, and preach that:

- The time is near
- The blow can come at any time
- We are living in a time of historic change very few are picking up on

Many think the big change will come with the physical second coming of Jesus Christ (and this, of course, is extremely important). Yet the Scriptures are clear that Jesus will reign at the right hand of the Father until the time comes for God to restore all things, as he promised through his holy prophets (Acts 3:21). Jesus will reign from heaven, until all his enemies are under his feet. The last enemy is death (1 Corinthians 15:25-26). The ministry of Elijah and Elisha is a prophetic picture of what will be accomplished prior to (and to set the stage for) the physical return of the Lord Jesus.

The Lord will have a people (the body of Christ) here on earth who will stand firm until their enemies are under their feet (Revelation 10:1-2). This is when Jesus will return (Revelation 11:15-19).

God has given much opportunity, and he isn't willing that any should perish. Yet Scripture states that the judgment begins from the house of the Lord (1 Peter 4:17-19).

The prophetic message regarding times and seasons of God is linked in Scripture to the agricultural year in Israel. There is a time to prepare the ground, a time to plant, a time to cultivate, a time to harvest the first fruits, and a time for the final harvest that includes the oil, wine, and wheat when everything must be harvested and secured or stored.

At harvest time, the fruit is evident. Bitter, corrupt, poisonous fruit that has nothing to do with God is unacceptable, and there's no time to plant something different in their hearts. The Lord won't give another opportunity if with their dying breath, they only desire to consult with demons regarding their prospects. This is why the Lord has a message for those who still have time.

We are entering into the great end-time harvest. Jesus said, *Ye shall know them by their fruits* (Matthew 7:16).

### Let us pray:

Heavenly Father, we ask that we may understand where we are in history, that we may be able to perceive the spectacular moment on the horizon for those who are clean and for those who desire to be clean.

May we be cleansed immediately, before the curtain falls on this stage of history. We ask this in the name of our Lord Jesus. Amen.

# Chapter Eight
## The Double Portion

The Lord is preparing to take away the things of the kingdom of the god of this world and place them into the hands of the true sons of God. This marks the true division of time.

> And the seventh angel sounded the trumpet, and there were great voices in the heaven, saying, The kingdoms of this world are reduced unto our Lord and to his Christ; and he shall reign for ever and ever. (Revelation 11:15)

On the fiftieth day after the passover, the Holy Spirit fell on the day of pentecost upon the early church (Acts 2). Gifts and ministries of God poured out for individuals and for the church under an anointing, which is symbolized by the anointing of the prophet Elijah. In 2 Kings 2 we find the secret of the difference between the single portion and the double portion. It's a huge difference.

This account describes the transition between the stage when the true servants of the Lord were mistreated, imprisoned, and martyred to a place of total victory in God.

Over the long history of the church, millions of God's true servants have been persecuted, banished, or killed. This includes people like Elijah who were nonconformists and refused to blindly follow those ruling over the people of God. And this persecution continues at a more intense pace today. Over the past twenty-five or thirty years, more men and women of God have been killed in Colombia than in any other country on the face of the earth. In terms of displaced persons, according to the United Nations, Colombia is second only to Syria. Why would this be?

The same spirit of intolerance present during pagan Rome and during the Inquisition is still alive, even though the human groups and sources causing the persecution vary. In the case of Colombia, it is only since WWII that any significant Bible distribution has taken place. The same is true in many other countries. Between 1948 and 1958, a large percentage of the evangelical Christians of Colombia were killed or displaced from their homes. Similar things have happened to Jews and Christians all over the globe for the past two thousand years. However, throughout this troubled history, a remnant with an anointing similar to that of Elijah has always remained.

Now we are at the time in history when God is about to pour out the double portion received by Elisha. Elijah himself walked in this anointing in 2 Kings chapters 1 and 2 prior to leaving. This is the anointing of grand victory, the anointing of not having to take even one step back.

In the second book of Kings, the prophets exhibited more power from God than what occurred in the first book of Kings. In circumstances when the prophet Elijah was forced to flee in 1 Kings, he was able to calmly face any situation in 2 Kings. The unclean king is now the one in trouble.

It's the king of the people of God, the king of Israel, who is on his deathbed and sends three groups of fifty soldiers to arrest Elijah. Two groups are destroyed, and when the third group displays the right attitude, they are spared.

Ezekiel shared a similar prophecy in which two-thirds of those linked with pentecost are cut off, and of the third part that remained, only those who have the right attitude survive (Ezekiel 5:1-4). This same type of thing is also mentioned in the book of Revelation.

At the time of division — which I am confident is very near — two-thirds of what belongs to pentecost is cut off, and only the third part continues. This third part consists of those who have the right attitude.

The third captain didn't arrive with a haughty, imperial attitude like that of his predecessors. He came on his knees, pleading for his life and for the lives of his fifty soldiers, because he knew Elijah had something different — that things had changed.

Elijah didn't move from the mountaintop until the LORD told him not to be afraid to go and tell the king he would not recover;

he would die. He wasn't sent to give a second chance to an evil king, who was the son of an evil king, who even when he was dying, decided to send his soldiers to arrest Elijah instead of consulting God.

In our natural state, even with gifts and ministries from God, we are all evil kings descended from evil kings and, therefore, have no business lording it over the people of God. In the kingdom of God, the servant of all is the greatest; the least is the greatest (Luke 9:48).

During these long years, lukewarm Christians have had little to fear from the church. They've taken communion, given tithes and offerings, and nothing much has happened to them as long as they went along with the flow. God overturned this during the last days of Elijah, and he is doing so now.

According to Scripture, in the great realm of the church of pentecost, only the third part will survive what is coming. They will be refined and enter into a new anointing. It is happening now. The status quo is being overturned, and the devil knows he has run out of time. For this reason, he will attack with all of his fury, but when he encounters a clean people of God, he will find them untouchable. However, God will use him to bring judgment upon things being done in the name of God, which are corrupt and unclean.

With this in mind, ask yourself, "where is the real danger, now?" It isn't for those who are clean, for those who are pure in heart and sincere toward God. No! The danger is for those who are lukewarm, mediocre, what many call carnal Christians — those who trust in doctrine and a corrupt religious system instead of having a direct, personal relationship with Father God under his discipline and correction (Revelation 3:15-16).

## 2 Kings 2

> [1] And it came to pass, when the LORD would take Elijah up into heaven by a whirlwind, that Elijah went with Elisha from Gilgal.

Gilgal (meaning a circle or wheel) is the site where the children of Israel entered into the Promised Land after exiting the wilderness and crossing the Jordan River. It is also the site of the second circumcision, which is symbolic of the circumcision of the heart, because the Lord desires to place his heart in us. Gilgal is the place of conversion.

> ² And Elijah said unto Elisha, Tarry here, I pray thee; for the LORD has sent me to Bethel. And Elisha said unto him, As the LORD lives and as thy soul lives, I will not leave thee. So they went down to Bethel.

Elisha had his heart set on the new thing coming (Isaiah 43:19) and wasn't willing to "tarry" at Gilgal.

Bethel means "House of God." This is where Jacob lay on the ground with God up above and received a great revelation. A ladder appeared between heaven and earth with angels ascending and descending. This is where Jacob made his famous vow to give God a tithe of all God gave him (Genesis 28:20-22). However, this vow wasn't enough to deliver Jacob from the revenge of Esau, his brother, who was on his way to kill him with four hundred men. He had to experience a face-to-face encounter with God at Peniel and make a total commitment to be able to face his enemy brother with confidence and win him over.

> ³ And the sons of the prophets that were at Bethel came forth to Elisha and said unto him, Knowest thou that the LORD will take away thy master from thy head today? And he said, Yes, I know it; be silent.

Why tell the prophets to be silent? Why not tell them to declare whatever they know about what the Lord is about to do?

We currently have prophets falling all over themselves in their eagerness to prophesy. At "Bethel," at the ten percent commitment level, it is teeming with prophets (or with prophecy teachers) who desire to go on record, foretelling what will happen next. They even have intricate charts and PowerPoints. Most of them are intrigued with the Bethel experience and would never consider leaving.

> ⁴ And Elijah said unto him again, Elisha, tarry here; for the LORD has sent me to Jericho. And he said, As the

LORD lives and as thy soul lives, I will not leave thee. So they came to Jericho.

"Tarry here."

Many desperately seek a word from a true prophet of God like Elijah, and they would be thrilled to stay at "Bethel" for the rest of their lives. Imagine them telling the testimony afterward of how "Elijah," or "John the Baptist," or whoever God may be using now told them to tarry at Bethel under the vow of Jacob with the ninety percent for me and ten percent for God mentality.

It is fine with God if someone desires to tarry at Bethel, but Elisha knew doing so would disqualify him from the fullness of the new day of God.

"Tarry here?" No Sir!

Elisha knew he couldn't tarry there, even with a direct personal word from the prophet Elijah. Why didn't Elisha follow the word of Elijah? Why didn't he remain at Bethel? Because God didn't give Elisha a direct personal word to stay.

This shines a light on the problem we have today. It is much easier to get words from a prophet or from many prophets than it is to pay the price of total commitment necessary to receive direct guidance from God. The direct Word of the LORD doesn't flow freely in the realm of the ten percent commitment.

If you decide to tarry in the realm of ten percent living, you must seek a pastor or group to tithe to. In turn, they will guarantee your prosperity in "Bethel" and be available to counsel every move you make.

If you study history, you'll find Bethel became so corrupt that God removed his presence. After initially being called the House of God by Jacob, it degenerated to the point that God completely abandoned it, and he never went back.

Those who desire to stick with the commitment of Bethel may continue to do so, but what we learn from Elisha's example is that he wasn't content to tarry at Bethel.

*So they came to Jericho ...* Jericho means "she has her own moon." Jericho was totally destroyed except for the house of the harlot Rahab. She and her family were saved because she hid the two spies of God and marked the window of her house with a scarlet thread. Jericho symbolizes another part of the religion of men. The moon represents the people of God (Israel and the church). In Jericho, however, they desired to have their own moon — to reflect their own light instead of the light of God.

Joshua pronounced a curse over anyone who would rebuild Jericho, but it was rebuilt in the days of King Ahab by Hiel the Bethelite at the cost of two of his sons (1 Kings 16:34). The past several decades have seen many modern-day Bethelites furiously rebuilding their own versions of Jericho with disastrous consequences for their children.

The church is like this when it follows the natural world. We think we are experiencing a great revival, a full moon, but it doesn't last. Instead, it continues to wane until there is nothing left. In fact, at times the church has gone into total eclipse as the "moon" comes between the sun and the earth causing a total blackout during what is supposed to be daytime. There have been times in which the church was so apostate and full of corruption that even non-Christian historians described it as the dark ages until the Renaissance and the Reformation, which let some light back in.

Elisha could have stayed in Jericho among those who build their own kingdoms above and beyond the commandments of God. Many places like this exist.

> ⁵ And the sons of the prophets that were at Jericho came to Elisha and said unto him, Knowest thou that the LORD will take away thy master from thy head today? And he answered, Yes, I know it; be silent.

If the ten percent commitment of Bethel won't suffice, there is ample space in Jericho for a bright new ministry to build an empire. Elisha would have been very well received in Jericho, but he told her prophets to be silent.

The coming realm isn't the realm of prophets who tell people things they don't perceive. Instead, it will be a new day in which only those who have a clean heart will be moved by God. They have direct access with the Lord and won't require the prophets of Bethel or Jericho.

The Lord Jesus didn't run around seeking confirmation from other prophets. (Jesus is the example for all of us). His heart was linked with the heart of his Father because he was clean. He was the temple of God, because his Father dwelt in him by the Holy Spirit.

This is what God has now for those who have a pure heart — those who have the presence of the Lord Jesus and his Father. They need not go through the hoops of the prophets of Bethel or of Jericho. This is linked to the spiritual fulfillment of the Day of Reconciliation or Atonement (Leviticus 23:27-32).

> 6 And Elijah said unto him, Tarry, I pray thee, here, for the LORD has sent me to the Jordan. And he said, As the LORD lives and as thy soul lives, I will not leave thee. And thus the two went on.

Remember this all began at Gilgal, which is the second circumcision of the children of Israel after their long journey through the desert, the desert of pentecost. This howling wilderness (of the seemingly "good" intentions of man) also represents the age of the church, as we have known it until now. In order to fully enter into the realm of victory, of the anointing which overcomes, of the anointing that rots and destroys the yoke of men, it is necessary to voluntarily go to the Jordan when God decides that it is time to fulfill the Day of Reconciliation (Leviticus 23:29). This was the only day in the year that the High Priest was authorized to enter the realm of the holy of holies behind the veil. Jesus is now our High Priest, and we may enter the throne room of the presence of God if we are hid in his life. This realm is by invitation only (Matthew 20:16; 22:14; Revelation 17:14).

Elijah and Elisha went to the Jordan, which prefigures the Day of Reconciliation.

The Jordan represents more than turning our back on the ten percent commitment of Bethel and the private kingdoms of Jericho. The Jordan is much more than a circumcision (second or otherwise). The Jordan signifies the actual death of the old man. The old man cannot inherit the kingdom of God, for flesh and blood cannot inherit the kingdom of God (1 Corinthians 15:50). The New Testament also makes it clear that Elijah entered the fullness of the kingdom of God, because he was present in the glory of God at the Mount of Transfiguration (Matthew 17:3; Mark 9:4).

> ⁷ And fifty men of the sons of the prophets went and stood in front of them afar off; and the two of them stood by the Jordan.

This is another reference to those of pentecost (the church) who aren't quite willing to pay the price of total surrender — death to the old man and all that the Jordan represents.

When the Lord Jesus went to the cross, according to the account of Matthew, only a few women followed from afar, and apparently Matthew was making his observation from even farther away (Matthew 27:55). Matthew didn't record some of the events told by John who stood at the foot of the cross.

The fifty prophets (representing the church of the age of pentecost) were standing afar off. In the modern day church, most won't teach you to give your life for the Lord, even though they give how-to seminars on just about everything else. Instead, their prosperity message tells people to receive the Lord, so it will go better at work; then the Lord will bless with health and money and help solve all of your problems. If you continue to have needs, you only have to continue to attend their meetings, participate in their rituals, and pay them your tithes and offerings. Then they promise the Lord will solve any problems that remain, as they grant you access to their full-time prayer line and counseling centers.

But do they teach anything about going to the Jordan? To the cross? Dying a slow and agonizing death? They don't talk about following the Lord until the actual death of the old man (the old nature) or how the Lord will use the circumstances of this life to finish off everything related to the old man and the old nature. Such things aren't included in their message at all. They don't preach this, because if they did, the multitudes wouldn't come to them.

Therefore, after Elisha told the fifty prophets to be silent, they came out and watched from afar. They wanted to see what was going to happen to Elijah and Elisha in the Jordan, but they didn't desire to enter into the Jordan themselves.

> ⁸ And Elijah took his mantle and wrapped it together and smote the waters, and they separated to one side and the other so that they both went over on dry ground.

When we make the commitment to follow the Lord no matter what — when we are covered by a blood covenant on God's terms — it is possible to walk right through death without even noticing it. The story of Enoch is similar. Scripture states that Enoch didn't see death. In Hebrews 11, Enoch is mentioned in the list of the heroes of the faith and at the end of the list it says, *and these all died* (Hebrews 11:13).

Prior to Jesus' work of redemption on the cross, the devil had the keys to death and Hades. According to the parable of the rich man and Lazarus, there were two compartments for the dead. In the first compartment, he had Abraham, all the patriarchs, and everyone else who looked forward to redemption. In the second were those who were lost, and there was an impassable gulf between them that still allowed them to talk back and forth (Luke 16:22-26).

But what happened to Enoch? According to Hebrews 11:13, he died, and yet in 11:5 we are told he didn't *see death* because he *pleased God*. He was taken directly into the presence of God. To understand this seemingly contradictive information, we must remember that death, which is described as Hades, is a place the devil held the keys to. However, Revelation 1:18 makes it clear that Jesus Christ now holds the keys. Until the redemptive work of Jesus Christ, even Abraham and the other patriarchs were held hostage by death in Hades until Jesus descended into Hades, led captivity captive, and ascended on high (Ephesians 4:8-10).

Hades is the first death. It differs from the lake of fire which is the second death and the real hell (Matthew 10:28; Revelation 20:14). Many English Bibles mistranslate and confuse Hades, the first death, with the lake of fire.

So why didn't Enoch go to the devil's jail in Hades when he died? Because he died in obedience, walking with God, and the devil couldn't hold him. This is another realm and is essentially the same thing that happened to Moses (Jude 9). Elijah is a similar case, and Elisha accompanied Elijah into the realm beyond the veil, as symbolized when he crossed the Jordan and then came back out on this side after re-crossing the Jordan by himself. In fact, when the children of Israel came into the Promised Land, they miraculously crossed the Jordan, presenting the same type of symbol.

The symbolic meaning shows that it isn't possible to receive the fullness of the kingdom of God in the life of the old man. The kingdom of God and the inheritance of the saints are for those who are part of the new man in Christ. We cannot fully say that old things have passed away and all things are made new until the old man is actually dead.

If we walk with Jesus Christ, led by the Spirit of God, he will take us past death. Elijah used his mantle to open the waters of the Jordan. This covering symbolized a direct relationship with God. This same mantle allowed Elijah to stand in the presence of God on the mountain of God and live (1 Kings 19:13). When Elijah and Elisha got to the Jordan (which is death), it opened for them, and they went through on dry ground.

Therefore, on the other side (the other side of death is the same as the other side of the veil), they were in what is symbolized by the holy of holies — the presence of God. They left this side and entered the place of total victory for the people of God on the other side of the Jordan. God will have a people who can enter there and also come back here. Elisha represents this. The last seven chapters of Ezekiel also shed light on this very same concept. Ezekiel's temple has no holy place; it only has an inside and an outside (Ezekiel 42-44).

The priests who contaminated the holy place and caused Israel to sin were all outside and couldn't enter the presence of God. Only one family of priests, the sons of Zadoc (meaning righteousness) were allowed to stand in the presence of God. They ministered unto the Lord and could also go out and have contact with the people outside.

> ⁹ *And when they had gone over, Elijah said unto Elisha, Ask what I shall do for thee before I am taken away from thee. And Elisha said, I pray thee, let a double portion of thy spirit be upon me.*

*And when they had gone over ...* They actually crossed over the Jordan for Elisha to be given the opportunity to make his request, and as stated earlier, Elijah means "God himself" in Hebrew. Elijah had a measure of the Spirit of God, and Elisha desired a double portion.

> ¹⁰ *And he said, Thou hast asked a difficult thing. If thou shalt see me when I am taken from thee, it shall be so unto thee, but if not, it shall not be so.*

Now that they were on the other side of the Jordan, things were critical. Elisha couldn't be distracted. He had to keep Elijah in his sight at all times.

In this symbolic example, what exactly does Elijah represent for us? He is the first portion. Elijah is the little or much that God has given us until now. The Word of God says that he who is faithful with little will be faithful with much. He who isn't faithful with a little, the little he has will be taken away (Matthew 25:20-30; Luke 16:10-13; 19:11-27). Elisha found himself in this situation in his walk with Elijah into this new dimension. It was all or nothing.

It is possible to tarry at Gilgal or to remain happy over at Bethel with a ten percent commitment. You can stay at Jericho, and nothing will immediately happen. But if you choose to go over to the other side of the Jordan when God grants the opportunity, this is no game. Anyone who enters the realm of the holy of holies and who is not covered, protected, and hidden within the life of Jesus Christ will be destroyed.

Nothing that is unclean can remain in the presence of God. This is why God banished Adam and Eve from his garden. This is why he put cherubim with a flaming sword at the entrance to the garden — to ensure they could never return on their own. The cherubim and flaming sword were embroidered on the veil separating the holy place from the holy of holies as a reminder, so no one in the holy place would ever decide to enter the holy of holies on their own. This is why the fifty prophets of Jericho were watching from afar. This only takes place at the moment of God's invitation and design.

Elijah had to do this, for *it is appointed unto men to die once and after this the judgment* (Hebrews 9:27). It was the appointed time for Elijah to go, but Elisha wasn't content to remain on this side of the Jordan.

> ¹¹ *And it came to pass, as they still went on and talked, that, behold, a chariot of fire with horses of fire separated the two, and Elijah went up into heaven in a whirlwind.*

It doesn't actually say Elijah went up to heaven in a chariot of fire. A chariot of fire came and separated Elisha from Elijah, and Elijah went up into heaven in a whirlwind. The chariots and horses of fire came from the presence of God, and a whirlwind represents the judgment of God (which is death to the old or natural man). Those who have their hearts set on the things of this world, on this side of the Jordan, will always fear death and the judgments of God.

Elisha didn't fear. He was clean and walking in righteousness. The presence of God came so near to him that he could see the fiery horses, chariots, and the whirlwind, and he was completely unscathed as Elijah disappeared up into heaven.

The presence of God will destroy anyone who is unclean. The whirlwind, symbol of judgment, elevated Elijah into heaven. For a person who is clean in the life of God, the judgment won't harm them. It will only elevate them to a higher place. God doesn't destroy the righteous along with the wicked.

*A chariot of fire separated the two...* The chariot of fire seems to be on the ground, not in the air, for it separated the two *and Elijah went up into heaven in a whirlwind...*

> ¹² *And as Elisha saw it, he cried, My father, my father, the chariot of Israel and the horsemen thereof. And he saw him no more, and he took hold of his own clothes and rent them in two pieces.*

Israel is one of the names of God. Israel can mean "he will rule (as) God," referring to Christ.

The devil wasn't able to hold Elijah and lock him up in Hades, because the chariot and horsemen of Israel intervened. Elijah went up to heaven in a whirlwind instead of down into Satan's prison in Hades (Hebrew *Sheol*) with the souls of those awaiting redemption.

> 13 And lifting up the mantle of Elijah that had fallen from him, he went back and stood by the bank of the Jordan.

The Lord divided the life of the prophet Elisha into two parts: before and after this tremendous encounter with the presence of God.

All of the New Testament apostles received their commission directly from the Lord Jesus Christ. Those who attempt to fulfill what the church has called the Great Commission without being commissioned directly by Jesus do so at their peril. It is impossible to have an apostolic ministry without having an encounter with the direct presence of God.

Today the term *apostle* is considered quaint or old-fashioned in some quarters. Some prefer to use the word *missionary*. Others misuse the word *apostle* to describe those who have elevated themselves or who have been elevated by human peers. Make no mistake; God is about to show a huge difference between those he has sent and those he did not send.

The ministry of Elisha is symbolic of what is about to happen. This will affect all of the people of God, because the Lord is about to make this division: before and after. This was the case with the ministry of John the Baptist who came in the spirit and power of Elijah to prepare the way for the Lord Jesus. This is also the case now, as the people of God are being prepared for the second coming.

Remember the presence of Moses and Elijah with Jesus on the Mount of Transfiguration? In the end, Moses and Elijah faded, and only Jesus was left as the Father spoke. The anointing of passover and pentecost will fade away as the second coming of Jesus Christ draws closer and closer.

The single portion is one thing. The double portion is another. When God unites his clean, double portion people with Jesus Christ as the head (Revelation 10), the anointing will be unlimited. This is total transformation.

> [13] And lifting up the mantle of Elijah that had fallen from him, he went back and stood by the bank of the Jordan.
>
> [14] And taking up the mantle of Elijah that had fallen from him, he smote the waters, and said, Where is the LORD God of Elijah? And when he smote the waters, they separated to one side and the other, and Elisha went over.

The new thing coming isn't different from Elijah. It is the same LORD God of Elijah but dispensing in another concentration, another level. This is also symbolic of something that happened after Jesus died and rose again. When he breathed on his disciples and said, *Receive ye the Holy Spirit* (John 20:22), he soon ascended into heaven in a fashion similar to Elijah.

After his death and resurrection, and even after his ascension, Jesus demonstrated he is able to go back and forth between the corrupt realm of this earth and the heavenly realm such as when he appeared to Saul of Tarsus on the Damascus road.

The devil has continued to reign over this world until now. Soon the Lord Jesus will return and the devil will be deposed. Jesus is now the head of a many-membered body of Christ and the second coming of Jesus Christ will affect the entire body, which involves us.

When his body on earth is victoriously bearing the good fruit he desires, he will physically return as the head in overwhelming power and glory accompanied by all his saints (Jude 14-15). The new day, however, may begin in a very subtle manner like the transition between 1 Kings and 2 Kings. A change happened and the king who ruled over places like Gilgal, Bethel, and Jericho didn't notice. He thought he could still send his soldiers to arrest Elijah, but a new day had already dawned.

We are at the beginning of the new day in God—at a tipping point in history—just like Elisha at the beginning of his double portion ministry.

> 15 And seeing him, the sons of the prophets who were at Jericho said, the spirit of Elijah rests on Elisha. And they came to meet him and bowed themselves to the ground before him.

The second coming also involves the coming of age of the royal body of Christ—a body composed of many members (Ephesians 4:13). Elisha symbolizes this. The fifty sons of the prophets at Jericho recognized this and worshipped Elisha. A similar situation occurred with Joseph and his brothers (Genesis 42:6).

> 16 And they said unto him, Behold now, there are fifty strong men with thy slaves; let them go and seek thy master; peradventure the Spirit of the LORD has taken him up and cast him upon some mountain or into some valley. And he said, Do not send them.

Why did they want to search for Elijah?

The fifty prophets, even the best of pentecost, now realized the anointing of Elijah was gone. The anointing of pentecost was gone. The anointing they had used for their gifts to function and for their ministries and prophecies was now gone (Ezekiel 46:17). This is why they all wanted to go search for "Elijah." But Elisha said not to send them!

Don't continue to seek what God was doing in the past. He won't repeat himself. From now on, it is necessary to cross the Jordan and experience a direct encounter with the glory of God. Those unwilling to die to the old man won't have the anointing or unction of the holy of holies, for the anointing of the gifts and ministries linked to the holy place is fading fast and will soon end.

> 17 But when they urged him until he was ashamed, he said, Send. They sent therefore fifty men, and they sought him for three days, but did not find him.

"Fifty" men identifies with pentecost, which also links it to the church. Jesus rose from the dead on the third day, and this is also a prophecy of the resurrection of the body of Christ on the beginning of the third millennial day (Revelation 20:4-6).

Many attempt to go back to the glory days of past revival, and even though these past revivals have made great contributions to our spiritual heritage, it is impossible for us to return to what God did in the past.

> [18] And when they came again to him (for he tarried at Jericho), he said unto them, Did I not tell you to not go?

We are entering a new day, and we won't be able to return to the old days even though we have many fond memories of all God has done in the past.

The anointing is tied to the mantle of Elijah, which represents the way in which God directly covered Elijah without the need for human intermediaries. From now on, only those proven faithful with a little will be given more. Only those who have gone with Elijah (God Himself) through the Jordan and have returned with the mantle of a direct heavenly commission will be given the double portion.

> [19] And the men of the city said unto Elisha, Behold, the seat of this city is good, as my lord sees, but the water is evil, and the ground barren.

This is the present state of the city of the religion of men. The water (the message that is flowing) is evil, and the ground is barren and unable to produce the fruit of the Spirit. The representation and things of God have been contaminated. Even those faithful to God have been forced to live in the midst of the rottenness and corruption.

But watch what will happen now:

> [20] Then he said, Bring me a new cruise and put salt in it. And they brought it to him.
>
> [21] And he went forth unto the springs of the waters and cast the salt in there and said, Thus hath the LORD said, I

have healed these waters; there shall be no more death or
barrenness in them.

²² So the waters were healed unto this day, according to
the word which Elisha spoke.

This double portion anointing will rally the people of God and bring about the fulfillment of many prophecies written throughout the Bible. The time is coming when we won't have to put up with impossible circumstances, for we'll be able to overcome corruption and infirmity.

The eldest son of each family in Israel was entitled to a double portion of the inheritance upon coming into maturity. Elisha means "God of the coming (one)" and is typed with receiving the double portion inheritance of the Spirit, which pertains to Jesus Christ. May we take the example of Elisha to heart and in God's timing become joint heirs with Christ (Romans 8:17).

Isn't this interesting? The ministry of Elisha is similar, yet very different, from the ministry of Elijah. It is the same Spirit, but more intense and with possibilities for victory that didn't exist before.

²³ Then he went up from there unto Bethel, and as he was
going up by the way, young men of the city came forth
and mocked him, saying, Go up, thou bald head; go up,
thou bald head.

Scripture refers to three basic stages of maturity (natural and spiritual): children who are to be under the law of their mother, young men who are to voluntarily submit to their parents until the coming of age (which for the Jews under the law was at thirty), and those who have come of age and attained the level of maturity required in order to receive an inheritance or to be in spiritual ministry.

At the time that this took place, the "young men" of the city refers to those between the ages of twelve and thirty. Spiritually, children are typed with passover and the age of the law, such as the children of Israel; and young people are typed with pentecost (the church) and the age of grace, which is ending.

The desire and purpose of God is to bring all of his people to maturity. Many examples in Scripture have to do with times and seasons relating to a final harvest. Immaturity is a necessary stage of development; however, it isn't to be an end in itself.

When the "young men" of Bethel (House of God) began to make fun of Elisha, someone who had definitely come to spiritual maturity, the consequences were very serious. In Hebrew *bald* means "without glory," and Elisha had just returned from a very close encounter with the glory of God — with Elijah's mantle and a double portion of the Spirit.

Those who remain in Bethel under the ten percent commitment never come to spiritual maturity. As a result, they never develop the perfect discernment that comes with maturity (perfection and maturity are the same word in Hebrew). Jesus said that anyone who spoke against him could be forgiven, but anyone who blasphemed the Holy Spirit wouldn't be forgiven in this age or in the next (Matthew 12:31-32; Luke 12:10).

> 24 And he turned back and looked on them and cursed them in the name of the LORD. And two bears came forth out of the forest and tore apart forty-two young men of them.
>
> 25 And he went from there to Mount Carmel, and from there he returned to Samaria.

It never even dawned on these "young men" that times had radically changed. It's sad that many people today (even elderly) in church remain at "Bethel" in a most deplorable state of immaturity, because they never went on with God.

Forty-two in Scripture is symbolic of what must be corrected in man. The children of Israel had forty-one camps in the wilderness and entered the Promised Land under the leadership of Joshua (Joshua in Hebrew is the same as Jesus in Greek) and pitched their forty-second camp after crossing the Jordan.

Forty-two is six (the number of man) multiplied by seven (the number of God). In our natural state, none of us can please God.

He isn't trying to make an alliance with the old man, because he wants it dead. Only two possibilities exist:

1. We can voluntarily place our lives on the altar and walk with Jesus in the way of the cross (like Elisha crossing the Jordan with Elijah), or
2. Continue to develop the old man (even using gifts and ministries from God for our own pleasure and forming our own kingdoms like Ahab and his sons).

The immature "young men" of "Bethel" (regardless of their actual physical ages) are about to have a head-on collision with "Elisha" and the glory of God. Those using God to get what they want are about to be separated from those who are willing to sacrifice their own lives to do what God wants.

The king was accustomed to killing prophets and jailing them according to his whims, but he had a head-on collision with Elijah. The young men of Bethel commonly mocked those who claimed there was a path to maturity and total victory (in Christ) and that this path would lead to the actual death of the old man (the old nature).

The true prophets of God have been jeered, mocked, persecuted, and killed for thousands of years, and the tables are about to turn.

### Let us pray:

Heavenly Father, we ask that we may be able to understand this message and participate in your new day. That, beginning in our hearts, we may come out from under the curse that affects the old man in Adam, so that the light of your new day of righteousness may shine through each and every one of us. Amen.

# Chapter Nine
## The Way Out of Edom and the Defeat of Moab

In the previous chapter, the Lord took Elijah into heaven while Elisha remained on earth, and Elisha asked for and received a double portion of the Spirit that was upon Elijah. This corresponds with God's desire to have a ministry that will represent him as he is. Elisha's example in Scripture is outstanding. Very few key individuals described in the Bible have absolutely no negatives recorded. Elisha, along with people like Joseph, Daniel, and Deborah, has this distinction.

### 2 Kings 3

> ¹ Now Jehoram, the son of Ahab, began to reign over Israel in Samaria the eighteenth year of Jehoshaphat, king of Judah, and reigned twelve years.

This verse offers some interesting details. Without getting into the meaning of the names, the numbers eighteen and twelve associated with these kings are linked with Israel and the church (the people of God) in Scripture. Twelve denotes spiritual childhood, such as with the children of Israel under the law, and eighteen signifies young manhood, such as the church under grace.

Jehoram was an evil king with a good point or two, and Jehoshaphat was a good king with a bad point or two. Israel and the church have had many leaders like this.

> ² And he did evil in the sight of the LORD, but not like his father and like his mother, for he put away the images of Baal that his father had made.

Jehoram's father, Ahab, went down in history as the most evil king Israel ever had, and his mother, Jezebel (who was still living at this time) was the personification of false, corrupt religion laced with idolatry and fornication.

> ³ Nevertheless, he cleaved unto the sins of Jeroboam, the son of Nebat, who made Israel sin; he did not depart from them.

Jeroboam didn't allow the people of Israel to go to Jerusalem to worship before the LORD during the three annual obligatory feasts of passover, pentecost, and tabernacles. Instead, he set up golden calves in Samaria and Bethel and established his own places of worship. Today, we have those who have set up doctrines designed to bypass the cross, circumvent the infilling of the Holy Spirit, and prevent people from coming to maturity in Christ. Why do they do this? In order to control the immature. In some places of worship, the people are so immature they are like spiritual fetuses linked to the mother religious system by an umbilical cord. They are still in the dark, being force-fed and, yes, their little hearts beat, but they have yet to be born again into the light.

Scripture states that the soul (or life) of the flesh is in the blood and that without the shedding of blood there is no remission of sin (Leviticus 17:11; Hebrews 9:22). God ordained Israel to make blood sacrifices in the temple at Jerusalem, because he wanted to impress them with the necessity of dealing with sin and the flesh. Even though it was impossible for the blood of bulls and goats to take away sin (Hebrews 10:4), this foreshadowed Jesus' supreme sacrifice when he died for us once and for all. Jesus is our Passover Lamb who died to take away our sin. It is only by the infilling of his Holy Spirit at pentecost that the church received the power to overcome sin, the world, and the devil. It is only by being born again into the life of Jesus (this is the true meaning of passover) that we may receive the Holy Spirit (the true meaning of pentecost) and produce the fruit of righteousness, the fruit of the Spirit, and come to maturity in Christ (passover).

Jeroboam replaced the true worship of God with the worship of golden calves (a form of humanism). Like Aaron and the children of Israel in the wilderness, he began cult worship of the very kind God wanted to destroy. The calves symbolize what is wrong with the old man—the carnal man. The worship of golden calves represents humanism and doctrines of men. God desires for us to put the deeds of the flesh to death by the Spirit, so we may live in the power of his resurrection life (Romans 8:13).

The sins of Jeroboam included isolating the people under his control, so they couldn't mix with anyone outside of his control. This included not allowing people freedom to be under God's control. Jeroboam set up his own places of worship, his own sacred holidays, his own liturgy or worship service format—all of which were in direct competition with what God ordained. This type of thing has also taken place repeatedly in the church over the past two millennia.

> 4 And Mesha, king of Moab, was a pastor and rendered unto the king of Israel one hundred thousand lambs and one hundred thousand rams, with the wool.
>
> 5 But it came to pass, when Ahab was dead, that the king of Moab rebelled against the king of Israel.

The king of Israel had another king under him who was supposed to pay him tribute. Today many religious organizations expect those at the bottom to pay tribute to those at the top. In many of these places, pressure is put on leaders to draw in more and more "lambs" and "rams" and "wool." The king of Israel not only demanded the sheep; he also required them to be fleeced and all the wool given over to him. Does any of this sound familiar?

This is another reason why rebellion and division are prevalent among the people of God. Church splits are often caused by fights over "sheep" and "wool" and "rams." In the face of such rebellion, the king of Israel marshaled his troops and sought allies.

> 6 And king Jehoram went out of Samaria the same time and numbered all Israel.
>
> 7 And he went and sent to Jehoshaphat, the king of Judah, saying, The king of Moab has rebelled against me; wilt thou go with me against Moab to battle? And he said, I will go up; I am as thou art, my people as thy people and my horses as thy horses.

Jehoram (and even Jehoshaphat) handled a number of things in the wrong way and seemed totally oblivious to a number of serious issues.

Under the Law of God, it wasn't up to the king to number the people belonging to the army of God. This was only to take place under God's initiative, at which time a silver coin was collected for each person numbered to symbolize they'd been redeemed. David got into trouble for numbering the people on his own initiative and without the redemption payment (Exodus 30:12; 2 Samuel 24).

Moab was the incestuous son of Lot, Abraham's nephew. His name means "of his own father" and is a symbol of certain religiosity, which looks up to human ministry as their "father" instead of having a direct personal relationship with God the Father.

The Scripture also clearly states that the kings of Israel weren't to trust in horses, which symbolize the power to do things in the flesh (Deuteronomy 17:16).

> ⁸ And he said, Which way shall we go up? And he answered, The way through the wilderness of Edom.

Jehoram thought he was too weak to face Moab alone and decided he needed more allies. He convinced Judah and Edom to go with him into battle. In order to do this, he chose to travel *through the wilderness of Edom*.

> ⁹ So the king of Israel went and the king of Judah and the king of Edom, and as they walked round about seven days' journey through the desert, there was no water for the host or for the beasts that followed them.

Edom represents those who build their own kingdoms instead of God's kingdom. The way of Edom is a wilderness (desert) with no "water." Water represents the Word of the LORD.

> ¹⁰ Then the king of Israel said, Alas! The LORD has called these three kings together, to deliver them into the hand of Moab!

The first reaction of the king of Israel was to blame the LORD when Jehoram was the one who decided to go the way of the wilderness of Edom!

> ¹¹ But Jehoshaphat said, Is there not a prophet of the LORD here, that we may enquire of the LORD by him? And one of the king of Israel's slaves answered and said, Here is Elisha, the son of Shaphat, who poured water on the hands of Elijah.
>
> ¹² And Jehoshaphat said, The word of the LORD is with him. So the king of Israel and Jehoshaphat and the king of Edom went down to him.
>
> ¹³ Then Elisha said unto the king of Israel, What have I to do with thee? Go to the prophets of thy father and to the prophets of thy mother. And the king of Israel said unto him, No, for the LORD has called these three kings together, to deliver them into the hand of Moab.

Who called these kings together? The king of Israel. And he did it without consulting the LORD. He wouldn't have considered doing so at this point if Jehoshaphat hadn't insisted. The king of Israel had a phobia and thought God was his enemy. Many people in Israel and in America and around the world hold similar subconscious thoughts today. They make their own plans without ever taking God into account, and when things start going wrong, their guilty conscience kicks in, and they fear God will cause something horrible to happen to them.

Jehoram, like his father Ahab before him, seemed unable to take responsibility for his actions. He failed to realize that if something bad happened to him as a result of his own plan, it was his fault — not God's.

As I travel around the world, I find many people, and even entire groups, who name the name of the Lord but behave like Jehoram. They come up with a plan of action on their own, and when things go well, they take the credit and believe the results are because God approves of them, their doctrine, and their plans and ideas. However, if things start to go sour and the church splits or they lose their job or they have other negative consequences, many blame God. They never even consider that their problems have come about because they've operated in the flesh and never really heard from God in the first place.

When Ahab (and later Jehoram) received one hundred thousand lambs and one hundred thousand rams along with all the fleeces every year, they thought they really had it together. However, when they, their people, beasts, and even their allies were all about to die of thirst, Jehoram thought God did this to them and wanted to deliver them over to their enemies. In a certain sense, God does allow all of us to reap what we have sown individually and corporately.

> [14] And Elisha said, As the LORD of the hosts lives, before whom I stand, surely, were it not that I regard the presence of Jehoshaphat, the king of Judah, I would not look toward thee nor see thee.

Elijah's opening line before King Ahab started in a very similar fashion: *As the LORD God of Israel lives, before whom I stand …*

> [15] But now bring me a minstrel. And when the minstrel played, the hand of the LORD came upon him;
>
> [16] and he said, Thus hath the LORD said, Make this valley full of ditches.
>
> [17] For thus hath the LORD said, Ye shall not see wind, neither shall ye see rain; yet this valley shall be filled with water, that ye may drink, both ye and your livestock and your beasts.

Elisha's new ministry began when he crossed back over the Jordan River into the realm of man's corruption after being very near the glory of the presence of God. The first thing he did was heal the waters of Jericho, which were corrupt and sterile.

For the church today, this symbolizes that God will have a clean ministry (even unto those who have taken part in a corrupt religious system, many of whom represented God in a bad and ugly manner). He will cause a pure, clean message to flow, which will cleanse and purify those who repent. This will bring about great change, but not like the rain, thunder, and lightning of the days of Elijah. It will be entirely different. God will simply cause "water" to flow in the wilderness. This literally happened to Elisha, and it happened spiritually when John the Baptist preached repentance in the wilderness in preparation for the ministry of Jesus. We are now, however, at the end of the church age, and God will once again cause the water of his Word to flow in the wilderness of man's seemingly good intentions.

In a certain sense, we are the wilderness God desires to fill with the water of the Word of his presence by the Holy Spirit. In previous revivals, there were huge meetings and spectacular outward manifestations of repentance and the miraculous presence and events sponsored by the Holy Spirit. This time, however, God is about to pour out his Spirit in the wilderness in a most quiet and powerful way.

> For thus hath the LORD said, Ye shall not see wind, neither shall ye see rain; yet this valley shall be filled with water, that ye may drink, both ye and your livestock and your beasts. (v. 17)

In the days of Elijah, it was possible to see the wind and rain, yet Elijah learned the true presence of the LORD wasn't in the wind, the fire, or the earthquake. Elijah confronted Ahab with a word from God, telling him that there would be no rain or dew except by his word. Now in the double portion ministry, Elisha is prophesying abundant water and that people won't even see the wind and the rain. Furthermore, even the "livestock" and the "beasts" will have their thirst satisfied. In what is coming, even those who aren't converted will have their thirst satisfied at least once. If they have any genuine doubts or questions concerning God, he will provide the answer.

> 18 And this is but a light thing in the sight of the LORD; he will also deliver the Moabites into your hands.

God's judgment will begin with the house of the LORD and take out those who are lukewarm (Revelation 3:16). Moab was a shirttail relative of Abraham who represented God the Father, the father of those who have faith, but according to the Law of God a Moabite wasn't allowed to enter the temple of God even to the tenth generation (Deuteronomy 23:3). Moab, meaning "of his own father," was the son of Lot by Lot's own daughter. This is a symbol of those who claim the church as their mother, but in reality, God isn't their father. They've been fathered by a human ministry and not by divine intervention.

In this biblical account, the Moabites gave occasion for the conflict because they insisted on retaining the new "lambs" and "rams" along with all the "wool" they had accumulated from fleecing the sheep. Even though Jehoram and the king of Edom had their problems and inconsistencies, God decided to lower the boom on Moab first.

We are rapidly approaching a time in history when the modern day Moabites will be in hot water. Some have stolen and fleeced sheep for many years and have appeared to be getting away with it. This is about to end. Here is what God decreed against them by the mouth of the prophet Elisha:

> [19] And ye shall smite every fenced city and every choice city and shall fell every good tree and stop every fountain of water and mar every good piece of land with stones.

The judgment of God is about to fall upon those calling themselves part of the people of God who aren't true sons of Father God. Their fenced, choice cities (congregations and even denominations) will be smitten. God will no longer allow them to have any "good" trees, "fountains" of water, or any arable "land." God will no longer allow his Word to flow and prosper in "Moab."

> [20] And it came to pass in the morning, when the present was offered, that water came by the way of Edom, and the land was filled with water.

What happens in the morning? A new day dawns.

What is the "present"? It is the work of our hands, which is only acceptable to God if we are in a proper covenant with him. Note: The Jubilee Bible translates this word properly beginning with Cain's offering in Genesis 4:3, and a pattern emerges throughout the Scripture. Each blood sacrifice was also to have a present (translated in other Bibles as grain offering). The work of our hands is only acceptable to God if we are in a blood covenant with him and the life of Jesus Christ is flowing through us instead of our own corrupt Adamic life.

We are at the time in history when a new day in God is dawning. In Scripture, it is the evening and the morning that make up the day (Genesis 1:5). It is out of the night of adversity, obscurity, and chaos that the new day dawns. This will be a big change.

In the morning, when the present was offered (by the Law there was a morning and an evening sacrifice and each was to be accompanied by a present), they were to sacrifice an animal and along with the lamb, the grain which was the work of their hands. Remember that Cain did this backwards and offered the work of his hands with no blood sacrifice and was therefore rejected (Genesis 4:3-5).

The true Lamb of God who takes away the sin of the world is Jesus Christ, and his sacrifice and the work of his hands (us if we allow him to work in and through us) is acceptable to God the Father. Therefore, the work of our hands is also acceptable to God, when we are in a blood covenant with Jesus Christ. This means our old man is to be considered dead and that Jesus Christ is to be alive *in* us by the power of the Holy Spirit (Colossians 1:26-28).

Over the centuries, many have lost the vision of the simplicity of the gospel, and it has taken some a long time to understand that it is only the life and work of Jesus Christ that is acceptable to God the Father. He desires to put the life of Christ in each of us, and when Christ reigns in us, the work of our hands, by the power of the Holy Spirit, is acceptable to God. It is then that we can do things for God which are ordained by God and accomplished by the resources of the Spirit of God which will influence the eternal destiny of many people (Ephesians 2:8-10).

On the other hand, if we invent our own good works, they cannot possibly save us or anyone else. Jesus, however, desires to work in our hearts, and after cleansing our hearts, he also desires to work through us.

> And it came to pass in the morning, when the present was offered, that water came by the way of Edom, and the land was filled with water. (v. 20)

The entire army had spent the night digging ditches, so they could receive the blessing of God when the new day dawned. Remember that many of the seven thousand who had not bowed their knee to Baal were undoubtedly part of that army. Where did the water of the Word and the blessing of God come from? It came by the way (out) of Edom. Edom is a symbol of building our own kingdoms instead of the true kingdom of God.

What does God desire of us? God desires that we place our lives upon the altar of God and open the way for the Holy Spirit to work in us. Then, when the blessing of God is poured out, we will be a vessel to contain it. God desires for us to leave Edom (the place of building our own kingdoms). It is on the way out of Edom that the water of the life of God will overtake us, if we recognize we are in trouble and seek him with all our heart.

When Elijah confronted the prophets of Baal, he spent a lot of time digging a trench around his sacrifice and pouring twelve pitchers of water over it, until it filled the trench containing the two measures of seed (1 Kings 18:32). Then Elisha had the entire army digging trenches as they prepared for the blessing of God! Exactly what does this mean and how does it apply to us?

When God sends the Holy Spirit to us, it is best that we be found empty; that we aren't found fooling around with other spirits that aren't holy; that our pride and selfishness be on the altar instead of reigning in our hearts. If we offer the "present" (the work of our hands) under the conditions God seeks, then he will bless us and break the curse, which has reigned from Adam until now. God says he will not reject those who come to him with a humble and contrite spirit. The present or work of their hands offered by this end-time army turned out to be a vast array of ditches in the wilderness!

*Water came by the way* [out of] *Edom* ... We must leave our own kingdoms behind, our own things and our own deeds, and when we get into the desert where there is nothing, we will die of thirst if the Lord doesn't intervene. But what does the Lord require from us? He requires that we listen to his voice, take heed, and open up space (inside of us) for him to act.

> ²¹ And when all the Moabites heard that the kings were come up to fight against them, they gathered all that were able to gird on a girdle and upward and stood in the border.
>
> ²² And when they rose up early in the morning, and the sun shone upon the water, and the Moabites saw the water before them as red as blood;
>
> ²³ and they said, This is blood: the kings are surely slain, and they have smitten one another. Now, therefore, Moab, to the spoil.

Moab had rebelled against Israel. They decided to keep the "lambs" and the "rams" and the "wool." Today we have congregations, groups of churches, and even synagogues that split along similar lines. The rebellious Moabites represent those individuals or groups who desire to be the (spiritual) fathers and have everyone depend on them instead of joining the people to the Lord.

When God sent waters of blessing, Moab made a fatal misinterpretation. God desires to change the water (of his Word) into the wine of his life. Jesus did this early in his ministry at the wedding of Cana (John 2:7-9). The Moabites thought the water in those trenches that brought life for the kings of Israel, Judah, and Edom was really blood. They misinterpreted life for death!

*Now, therefore, Moab, to the spoil.* It wasn't enough to keep the one hundred thousand lambs, the one hundred thousand rams and all the wool; no, now they wanted the spoil, also.

God is about to work in such a way that each person reaps the desires of their heart. Those who have the heart of God and desire to see gain for the kingdom of God will live to see it, and those who desire to control and spoil everyone else will fall into their own trap.

> ²⁴ But when they came to the camp of Israel, the Israelites rose up and smote the Moabites so that they fled before

them, but they went forward smiting the Moabites, even in their country.

<sup>25</sup> And they beat down the cities, and on every good piece of land each man cast his stone and filled it, and they stopped all the fountains of water and felled all the good trees until they left their stones only in Kirharaseth, for the slingers went about it and smote it.

Kir-haraseth, the capital of Moab, means "brick town." Today the religious system controlled by "Moabites" is like a brick factory. If you desire to participate in this system, you must jump through all the hoops. In order to be baptized, you must go to a baptismal or new members' class. In order to be married, there is another obligatory approved course to take. In order to be a leader, many man-made requirements must be followed regarding education, theology, and doctrine. Some "Moabites" even require a person to take a seminar called Life in the Spirit in order to "receive" the Holy Spirit! Those who don't pass such courses don't meet the requirements and aren't allowed to go on to the next level. Each person is given exactly the same form to follow, just like making identical bricks at a brick factory, as if the work of the Holy Spirit can be controlled or shaped by traditions of men. This is Kirharaseth.

On the other hand, when God builds, he uses living stones. He forms each unique stone by his own hand, and no two stones exactly alike. The Lord will build his temple from these living stones with each stone designed and crafted by him for a specific place and purpose. He won't use a hammer or any iron tool (symbolic of legalism) when he brings his true temple together. He has planned and worked on individual stones for more than six thousand years.

> … they left their stones only in Kirharaseth, for the slingers went about it and smote it. (v. 25)

This seems to indicate the "slingers" also used the bricks for their sling catapults and shot them at the city of Kirharaseth until only stones too big for them to use for ammunition remained around the city. When the judgment of God falls on the land of "Moab," only the true stones of God will remain.

> ²⁶ And when the king of Moab saw that the battle was overcoming him, he took with him seven hundred men that drew swords to break through unto the king of Edom, but they could not.

Seven hundred seems to be a significant number and here it represents the perfection of the plans of the king of Moab. He made one last desperate attempt to break through to the king of Edom (Edom represents those who build their own kingdoms) and failed.

We are entering a time when the judgments of God are beginning to fall. When God decides someone or something won't prevail, they will fail no matter how seemingly good their plans or how abundant their resources.

Until now, the wheat and the tares have grown together in the same field. The sun has shined and the rain has fallen upon those who are good and those who are evil. Now, however, God is bringing some of his people into a new day of "double portion" ministry in which some of the old rules will change.

When Elijah confronted the prophets of Baal and the true fire fell from heaven, Elijah told the people not to let the prophets of Baal escape. Now Elisha had the kings and armies of three entire nations helping to bring about God's judgments upon Moab. The prophetic judgment upon the land of Moab declares that:

> Ye shall smite every fenced city and every choice city and shall fell every good tree and stop every fountain of water and mar every good piece of land with stones. (v. 19)

Any true living stones of God who are still in the religious land of Moab will be saved; everything else will be dealt with when the judgments of God fall.

> ²⁷ Then he took his eldest son that should have reigned in his stead and offered him for a burnt offering upon the wall. And there was great indignation in Israel, and they departed from him and returned to their own land.

The king of Moab is similar in some ways to the devil who attempts to beguile religious people by telling them they are going to receive the prosperity of this world and reign over the world like kings. In many religious places, the Holy Spirit is no longer present. Instead, another spirit, a spirit of greed, which is a form of idolatry, has taken over and the devil who is behind this entices people by telling them they can have the best of this world and heaven to boot (Colossians 3:5).

The devil, however, is a very poor loser. When he sees that he's lost the battle, he will be capable and willing to sacrifice his own sons — those he promised would reign. Scripture is clear that the tares are the sons of the evil one. When the devil sees his immediate destiny is to be bound for a thousand years with the chains of death in the bottomless pit (Revelation 20:1-3), he will very likely start sacrificing his own sons if he thinks it may help slow his own demise. This, of course, will be followed by final judgment and his eternal perdition in the lake of fire at the end of the thousand years (Revelation 20:7-10).

Six thousand years of recorded human history have passed. During that period, people have had opportunities to make deals with the devil and receive the benefits of this world in exchange for selling their soul. This doesn't just happen in the realm of the occult. Much of this has infiltrated Israel and the church by people who desire to control and manage the people of God in the same way they control and manage the things of this world.

This is what is behind Moab and Kirharaseth — the great city of the religion of men, built out of identical bricks. In other examples from Scripture, Babylon and the Tower of Babel were made of bricks (Genesis 11:3). God doesn't build in this manner. In fact, he delivered the children of Israel from making bricks as slaves of Pharaoh (Exodus 1:14; 12:51).

The devil isn't going to consolidate the kingdoms of this world and reign from a one-world government. He has tried to do this for six thousand years, but his kingdom is divided against itself and therefore cannot stand; it continues to fray and fragment (Matthew 12:25-26). When the devil makes his last stand, he will think nothing of killing his own sons. This is how it will end:

> He (Jesus) answered and said unto them, He that sows the good seed is the Son of man; the field is the world; the

good seed are the sons of the kingdom, but the tares are the sons of the wicked; and the enemy that sowed them is the devil; the harvest is the end of the age, and the reapers are the angels.

As therefore the tares are gathered and burned in the fire, so shall it be in the end of this age. The Son of man shall send forth his angels, and they shall gather out of his kingdom all things that offend and those who do iniquity

and shall cast them into the furnace of fire; there shall be wailing and gnashing of teeth. Then shall the righteous shine forth as the sun in the kingdom of their Father. He who has ears to hear, let him hear. (Matthew 13:37-43)

Those deceived by the promises of the devil will soon realize his promises aren't only false, but they lead to death (and perdition). All the people who, in the name of God, have gone after the prosperity of this world with the devil driving them and promising them more and more power and money may not even receive what's been promised. In the end they will lose their own souls and their eternal inheritance. They will not reign.

On the other hand, the Lord Jesus Christ will inherit all things, and we may stand firm in him if we are willing to turn our back on our own life and renounce the deeds of the flesh, the world, and the devil.

Scripture states: *If we suffer* [with him] *we shall also reign with him* (2 Timothy 2:12).

All who have ever followed the Lord Jesus have been counted as enemies of this world and of the world system. All who have remained true to the Lord throughout history have suffered persecution. The Lord is about to invert these things.

### Let us pray:

Heavenly Father, we thank you for the time you have given us. Thank you for sending us true prophets. We ask that we may be among your remnant in the midst of the great changes you are about to cause to take place. We ask this in the name of our Lord Jesus. Amen.

# Chapter Ten
## The Sons of the Prophets

We can learn from the success and failure of others. Lessons from accounts in the Bible all pertain to us. They are prophetic. God used the Israelites of old to show what would happen afterward in the Christian church.

The Christian church has often followed the same path as the Israelites. God blessed the generation that walked with him. Yet their children almost always, in the midst of great blessing and prosperity, turned their backs on God. This is the cycle.

In the New Covenant, if we are born again from above by the Spirit of God, we are part of the royal line of Jesus and therefore royalty. Jesus wants to prepare us to take responsibility as prophets, priests, and kings who will be used by God.

Consider the huge prophetic change that took place between the books of First and Second Kings. Similarly, in the church, the Lord first promises to give us the earnest or down payment of the inheritance (2 Corinthians 1:22; 5:5; Ephesians 1:13-14). Then after a certain time, God promises the fullness of the inheritance.

If we are legitimate sons of God who have received the earnest and are faithful with it, the day will come when we will receive the fullness. Jesus said that those who are faithful with a little will be faithful with much, while those who are unfaithful with a little, what little they have will be taken from them (Luke 16:10; Matthew 25:29).

The last true prophet of 1 Kings, Micaiah (a fuller form of Micah, meaning "who is like unto the LORD"), had a difficult task. He stood in the midst of hundreds of false prophets who told King Ahab that he could go and fight with the enemy and everything would turn out fine. The true prophet started to say the same thing but then had to speak the truth. God had ordered a lying spirit to deceive all of King Ahab's prophets except one.

This is very similar to what has happened here in Colombia and around the world. Prophets with a lying spirit are loose in the church, prophesying that things will go well for the natural man, prophesying that you may obtain the things of this world in a way contrary to God's way, prophesying that lukewarm, carnal, defeated Christians will be safely whisked off to heaven in a secret rapture before the great tribulation comes.

True prophets, on the other hand, say only what the Lord Jesus is saying. Jesus is saying that if we follow him, we must take up our cross daily (Luke 9:23). Jesus is saying that if we are willing to lose our life for him and for the cause of the gospel, we will find it (Mark 8:35). If we suffer with him, then we will also reign with him.

In the book of 2 Kings, the prophetic ministry never has to back up or retreat. They are never defeated or imprisoned. Some kings are good, some are bad, some are so-so; but the prophetic ministry doesn't just have the earnest of the anointing. They have enough of the fullness of the Spirit of God that no one can move them or prevail against them.

This is beginning to happen at this very moment today. We are crossing the same line — a line that will distinguish before and after. There continues to be all manner of people — good, bad, and so-so. Some dominate others, but those who truly represent the Lord are of another caliber.

Elisha is a symbol of this ministry. Elisha asked for a double portion of the Spirit or anointing of Elijah. The difference is very noticeable. Elisha never had to run and never made decisions based on the fear of man.

God will now have a people like Elisha — chosen — who have known God's presence and have come forth to minister to those who live in the darkness and shadows. We must also remember that even with his unlimited anointing, Jesus was still willing to lay down his life for us at the request of his Father. This is how he redeemed us. We may be asked to lay down our lives for our brethren or to reach our enemies (Revelation 11:7). If this should happen, God is very capable of taking care of our family.

## 2 Kings 4

¹ Now a certain woman of the wives of the sons of the prophets cried unto Elisha, saying, Thy slave, my husband, is dead; and thou knowest that thy slave feared the LORD; and the creditor is come to take my two sons to be his slaves.

² And Elisha said unto her, What shall I do for thee? Tell me what thou hast in the house? And she said, Thy handmaid has nothing in the house except a flask of oil.

This can obviously be interpreted on a personal level, but in Scripture a woman can symbolize a people, a nation, or the church. Bible prophecy always describes the people of God as a woman. This "woman" had a husband who was a servant of God, but he died and left his family in debt, and his sons were about to be placed into bondage. The only thing left was a flask of oil. This represents a limited anointing — a very limited portion of the grace of God.

³ And he said, Go, borrow vessels from all thy neighbours, empty vessels; borrow not a few.

Who are we? Scripture calls us vessels.

The prophet told the widow to find as many empty vessels as possible. Vessels must be completely empty because what the Lord is going to do won't work if we are full of ourselves.

⁴ Then enter in and shut the door upon thee and upon thy sons and pour out into all those vessels, and as each one is full, set it aside.

⁵ So she went from him and shut the door upon her and upon her sons, who brought the vessels to her, and she poured out the oil.

⁶ And when the vessels were full, she said unto her son, Bring me yet another vessel, And he said unto her, There are no more vessels. Then the oil stopped flowing.

⁷ Then she came and told the man of God. And he said, Go, sell this oil and pay thy debtors and live thou and thy sons on the rest.

This is a different anointing; this is enough to fill all of the empty vessels. God pours out enough grace to pay every debt and to supply all future need. This is what God will do now, but there are conditions; this anointing flows quietly behind closed doors, into clean, empty vessels until they are full and all needs are met (Matthew 6:1-6).

Notice the progression of the double portion Elisha ministry. First, he healed the corrupt waters and barrenness of Jericho. Then he had the entire army prepare to receive the blessing of the Water of the Word by digging trenches in the wilderness, and they repented and recognized their desperate need as they left by the way (out) of Edom (meaning doers or those who build their own kingdoms). The water was then turned red (symbol of the wine of the life of Christ) and this led to a tremendous victory over Moab (symbol of those who are of their own father — those who are not sons of the real Father). Oil flowed in the house of a widow woman who lived among the sons of the prophets, and this anointing filled all the empty vessels, delivered the entire household from bondage, and met every future need. This was the anointing that destroyed the yoke (Isaiah 10:27). Oil and wine are the symbols of the Feast of Tabernacles — the feast of fullness and resurrection life. This represents the transition into the kingdom age that will transpire after the first resurrection (Revelation 20:4).

## Resurrection Life

⁸ And it also happened that one day Elisha passed through Shunem, where there was an important woman, and she constrained him to eat bread, And so it was, that as often as he passed by, he turned in there to eat bread.

⁹ And she said to her husband, Behold now, I perceive that this is a holy man of God, who passes by us continually.

¹⁰ Let us make a little chamber, I pray thee, on the wall, and let us set for him there a bed and a table and a stool and a lampstand so that when he comes to us, he shall turn in there.

God ordered a pagan widow woman to sustain Elijah. A woman also sustained Elisha, but this woman was a well-connected Israelite who had a husband. This woman was from Shunem, meaning "to rest or to be quiet." The modern day Elisha company is sustained by a very special "woman" (representing clean people of God).

> 11 And it came to pass one day that he came there, and he turned into the chamber and slept there.
>
> 12 Then he said to Gehazi, his servant, Call this Shunammite. And when he had called her, she stood before him.
>
> 13 And he said unto Gehazi, Say now unto her. Behold, thou hast been diligent for us with all this care; what shall I do for thee? Dost thou have need that I speak for thee unto the king or to the captain of the host? And she answered, I dwell among my own people.

This woman, however, had a very special need. She was barren. Many of God's special people today are spiritually barren and sense this very same need to be fruitful.

> 14 And he said, What then shall we do for her? And Gehazi answered, Verily she has no child, and her husband is old.
>
> 15 Then he said, Call her. And when he had called her, she stood in the door.
>
> 16 And he said, At the appointed time, according to the time of life, thou shalt embrace a son. And she said, No, my lord, thou man of God, do not deceive thy handmaid.
>
> 17 But the woman conceived and gave birth to a son at the appointed time that Elisha had said unto her, according to the time of life.

Several important biblical accounts involve key men of God born of sterile women. This was the case with Samuel and John the Baptist.

> 18 And when the child was grown, it came to pass one day, that he went out to his father to the reapers.

This happened at harvest time. Today, we also find ourselves in the season of the promised end-time harvest.

> <sup>19</sup> And he said unto his father, My head, my head. And he said to a servant, Carry him to his mother.
> <sup>20</sup> And when he had taken him and brought him to his mother, he sat on her knees until noon and then died.

This only child is destined to be the heir. Yet he cannot come into the inheritance in his own life or under his own headship. Something in each of us must die if we are to come to maturity in Christ. At twelve years old, under the Law, the child is accountable but not mature.

> <sup>21</sup> Then she went up and laid him on the bed of the man of God and shut the door upon him and went out.
> <sup>22</sup> And calling her husband, she said, Send me, I pray thee, one of the young men and one of the asses, that I may run to the man of God and come again.
> <sup>23</sup> And he said, Why must thou go to him today? It is neither new moon nor sabbath. And she said, Peace.

This crisis was personal and she didn't want to upset her husband. She knew in her heart exactly what to do, and there was no time to waste.

> <sup>24</sup> Then she caused the ass to be saddled and said to her servant, Lead and go forward; slack not the pace for me except I bid thee.
> <sup>25</sup> So she went and came unto the man of God to Mount Carmel. And it came to pass, when the man of God saw her afar off, that he said to Gehazi, his servant, Behold, yonder is that Shunammite.
> <sup>26</sup> Run now, I pray thee, to meet her and say unto her, Dost thou have peace? And thy husband? And the child? And she answered, Peace.

This is the second time that she said, "peace."

27 And when she came to the man of God in the mountain, she caught him by the feet. And Gehazi came near to thrust her away; but the man of God said, Let her alone, for her soul is bitter within her; and the LORD has hid it from me and has not revealed it to me.

28 Then she said, Did I desire a son of my lord? Did I not say, Do not deceive me?

29 Then he said to Gehazi, Gird up thy loins and take my staff in thy hand and go; if thou meet anyone salute him not; and if anyone salutes thee, answer him not again, and lay my staff upon the face of the child.

The staff of Elisha is a symbol of the discipline and authority of God. The child must come under the direct authority of God.

30 Then the mother of the child said, As the LORD lives and as thy soul lives, I will not leave thee. And he arose and followed her.

31 And Gehazi had gone on before them and had laid the staff upon the face of the child, but there was neither voice, nor attention. Therefore he went again to meet him and told him, saying, the child is not awaked.

Gehazi was a very gifted servant like many Christians today. Gehazi, however, received orders from Elisha and not directly from God. In some situations only a direct word from the LORD will suffice. Only a direct word from the LORD will provide the grace for us to be victorious.

32 And when Elisha was come into the house, behold, the child was laid dead upon his bed.

33 He went in therefore and shut the door upon both of them and prayed unto the LORD.

Prayer, in the highest sense, is two-way communication with the LORD.

34 Then he went up and lay upon the child and put his mouth upon his mouth and his eyes upon his eyes and his

hands upon his hands; thus he stretched himself upon the
child; and the flesh of the child waxed warm.

³⁵ Then he returned and walked through the house to and
fro and went up and stretched himself upon him again;
and the child sneezed seven times, and the child opened
his eyes.

In a similar case, Elijah stretched himself upon a dead child three times and the child revived. In these two cases, however, we find similarities and differences. It isn't enough just to do exactly what worked last time for someone else. We must have a fresh word from the LORD for each new situation.

³⁶ And he called Gehazi and said, Call this Shunammite,
So he called her. And as she was coming in unto him, he
said, Take up thy son.

³⁷ Then she entered in and fell at his feet and bowed herself
to the ground and took up her son and went out.

It is interesting to note that the apostle Paul had a similar experience in the New Testament. A young man fell asleep during one of Paul's messages, as it went late into the night, and he fell from a third story window (Acts 20:9,10).

³⁸ And Elisha returned to Gilgal. Then there was famine in
the land; and the sons of the prophets were sitting before
him, so he said unto his servant, Set on the great pot and
make pottage for the sons of the prophets.

³⁹ And one went out into the field to gather herbs and
found a wild vine and gathered his lap full of wild grapes
and came and shred them into the pot of pottage, for they
knew them not.

Jesus said that he is the vine and we are the branches; if we abide in him, we shall bear good fruit. The grapes and wine that come from his vine bring life. However, wild grapes symbolize the life of the natural man. If we feed on our own life or attempt to feed others with that which comes from the old life of Adam, there will be death in the pot.

> ⁴⁰ So they poured out for the men to eat. And it came to pass, as they were eating of that pottage, that they cried out and said, O thou man of God, there is death in the pot. And they could not eat it.
> ⁴¹ But he said, Then bring meal. And he cast it into the pot, and he said, Pour out for the people that they may eat. And there was no evil thing in the pot.

Meal is ground up grain. The grain offering or present represents the work of our hands. This is acceptable to God if we are in a blood covenant with him. Elisha was in a right covenant with God, and those who ate were all sons of the prophets; therefore the work of their hands was acceptable to God. Jesus even said that if any of those who believe in him should drink any deadly thing, it shall not hurt them (Mark 16:18).

> ⁴² Then a man came from Baalshalisha, who brought the man of God bread of the firstfruits, twenty loaves of barley, and full ears of wheat in the head. And he said, Give unto the people that they may eat.
> ⁴³ And his minister said, How can I set this before one hundred men? He said again, Give the people, that they may eat, for thus hath the LORD said, they shall eat, and some shall be left over.
> ⁴⁴ So he set it before them, and they ate, and some was left over, according to the word of the LORD.

Barley and first fruits link this to pentecost, but it mentions one hundred men (instead of fifty during the days of Elijah). The number *one hundred* is symbolic of the plan of God. This is a double portion of pentecost, which provides enough for everyone until there is some left over. This is what happened when Jesus fed the five thousand and the four thousand.

This took place among the "sons of the prophets" during a time of famine. We know that in our time the real famine is of a spiritual nature related to hearing the words of the LORD (Amos 8:11). God will provide ample provision through an Elisha company for everyone among the "sons of the prophets" who are in a right covenant with God.

Soon after Elijah fled from Jezebel to the mountain of God, he learned that the presence of God wasn't in the wind, the earthquake, or the fire. It was in the still, small voice (1 Kings 19:11-12). Many think that because they don't see the wind, earthquake, or fire, they don't have the Holy Spirit or the Holy Spirit is not present.

We were in a meeting with Brother George Warnock in Bogotá a decade ago, and a woman left in a rush. Just before she went out the door, she exclaimed to my wife that she felt compelled to leave because there was no anointing in the meeting. For me, as the interpreter, even though Brother George was speaking in a soft voice, the presence of God was so powerful that I could hardly talk.

**Let us pray:**

Heavenly Father, we ask for clarity to discern the time we are in. We ask for courage to stand firm in your word instead of in our own. We ask that faith, hope, and love will reign in our hearts when the world around us is shaken and when those who are not on solid footing begin to fall.

May we administer that which we have according to your ways, so we may be among those who will reclaim the true inheritance. Amen.

# Chapter Eleven
## God Heals Naaman, the Enemy General

### 2 Kings 5

¹ Now Naaman, captain of the host of the king of Syria, was a great man with his master and in high esteem because by him the LORD had given salvation unto Syria; he was also a mighty man in valour, but he was a leper.

The LORD can extend salvation to anyone at any time, and sometimes he uses people to accomplish his work—people who seem highly unlikely to us. In this passage, the LORD used Naaman to save his nation, even while his nation was hostile toward Israel, the people of God. God knew a lot about Naaman and called him *a mighty man in valor*. In fact, I wonder if Naaman could have been the certain man who, *shooting his bow in perfection, smote the king of Israel between the joints of his mail* (1 Kings 22:34)?

Naaman, however, seemed to know next to nothing about God. In Scripture, leprosy is symbolic of terminal sin. In the ancient world, leprosy was incurable, and so was sin prior to the advent of Jesus Christ.

² And the Syrians had gone out by companies and had brought away captive out of the land of Israel a little maid, and she waited on Naaman's wife.

³ And she said unto her mistress, if my lord would ask the prophet that is in Samaria, he would remove his leprosy.

The little girl had been captured and enslaved, but her faith in God remained strong. She displayed the same attitude shown by Daniel and his friends when they established a good relationship with difficult King Nebuchadnezzar. They accepted their situation as the will of God and displayed a good attitude towards their captors. This set the stage for God to work in the lives of their enemies.

This little girl had such a good testimony that Naaman, the enemy general, believed her.

> ⁴ And Naaman went in and told his lord, saying, Thus and thus said the maid that is of the land of Israel.
>
> ⁵ And the king of Syria said, Go, depart, and I will send a letter unto the king of Israel. And he departed, and took with him ten talents of silver and six thousand pieces of gold, and ten changes of raiment.

This was a lot of money. Ten talents of silver and ten changes of raiment refer to whatever Naaman thought it would take legally to be covered and redeemed. Six thousand pieces of gold shows that he thought he was perfect in his human righteousness (yet this is really self-righteousness). Naaman was willing to go through all the proper channels. He obtained a letter of endorsement from his boss, addressed to the enemy king of Israel who happened to be the son of King Ahab, whom Naaman had been instrumental in killing and defeating.

> ⁶ And he also took the letter to the king of Israel, which said, Now when this letter is come unto thee, behold, I have therewith sent Naaman, my slave, to thee, that thou may remove his leprosy.

In Israel they considered a leper, for all practical purposes, to be as a dead man.

> ⁷ And when the king of Israel read the letter, he rent his clothes and said, Am I God, to kill and to give life, that this man sends unto me to remove the leprosy of this man? Therefore now consider and see how he seeks a quarrel against me.

Did the king of Israel tear his clothes because he realized Naaman was most likely the man who had shot his father?

To help us understand the situation, think of it this way. Today, the king of Israel may represent the leader of a great church or of a great nation that is in trouble because their enemies in the world seem to have the upper hand (today the people of God have serious enemies that are once again threatening Western Christian civilization).

So, what if a top enemy leader responsible for a lot of havoc came to be cleansed of his sickness and sin? The king of Israel didn't even remotely consider the possibility of such a victory. He thought this was another enemy tactic. He completely failed to see the wonderful opportunity God placed before him, because he lacked faith and spiritual vision.

> 8 And when Elisha, the man of God, heard that the king of Israel had rent his clothes, he sent to the king, saying, Why hast thou rent thy clothes? Let him come now to me, and he shall know that there is a prophet in Israel.

Even though the corrupt king of Israel was full of unforgiveness and harbored desires for revenge, even when he misrepresented God and had mixed paganism with the things of God, Elisha's attitude demonstrated the real nature of God. Elisha wasn't bitter against the king of Israel, and he wasn't bitter towards the Syrian general. He stood apart from the conflict and only desired to demonstrate that true prophetic ministry was alive in Israel.

Who is a true prophet? One who speaks on behalf of God and says whatever God wants said regardless of circumstance.

> 9 So Naaman came with his horses and with his chariot and stood at the door of the house of Elisha.
>
> 10 And Elisha sent a messenger unto him, saying, Go and wash in the Jordan seven times, and thy flesh shall be restored, and thou shalt be clean.

Elisha knew quite a bit about the Jordan (symbol of death). God had a plan, and in that plan, he used Elisha to attack the pride and self-righteous arrogance of Naaman.

> 11 But Naaman went away angry and said, Behold, I thought, He will surely come out to me and stand and call on the name of the LORD, his God, and strike his hand over the place and remove the leprosy.

> [sup]12[/sup] Are not Abana and Pharpar, rivers of Damascus, better than all the waters of Israel? May I not wash in them and be clean? So he turned and went away in a rage.
>
> [sup]13[/sup] Then his slaves came near and spoke unto him, and said, My father, if the prophet had bid thee do some great thing, would thou not have done it? How much rather then, when he saith to thee, Wash and be clean?
>
> [sup]14[/sup] Then he went down and dipped himself seven times in the Jordan, according to the word of the man of God; and his flesh came again like unto the flesh of a little child, and he was clean.

In typical Elisha fashion, he didn't grandstand but sent a messenger. He focused everything on the LORD and on the Word of the LORD. He didn't compete at any level for the glory of God — a significant characteristic of the Elisha ministry.

> [sup]15[/sup] And he returned to the man of God, he and all his company, and came and stood before him, and he said, Behold, now I know that there is no God in all the earth, but in Israel. Now therefore, I pray thee, take a blessing from thy slave.
>
> [sup]16[/sup] But he said, As the LORD lives, before whom I stand, I will receive none. And he urged him to take it, but he refused.

Here we see a second vital characteristic of the Elisha ministry. He didn't seek money or any other form of earthly gain. The sons of the prophets had needs, but God supplied everything, even their food, on a daily basis. The purpose of Elisha was to clearly demonstrate to Naaman that God's grace, healing, and salvation were free.

In many religious environments today, what would happen if a powerful foreign stranger who was grateful for being healed by the LORD stopped at the door with ten talents of silver, ten changes of clothing, and six thousand pieces of gold?

> [sup]17[/sup] Then Naaman said, Shall there not then, I pray thee be given to thy slave two mules burden of earth? For from

now on thy slave will offer neither burnt offering nor sacrifice unto other gods, but unto the LORD.

¹⁸ In this thing may the LORD pardon thy slave, that when my master goes into the house of Rimmon to worship there, and he leans on my hand, if I also bow myself in the house of Rimmon, that the LORD pardon thy slave in this thing, if I bow down myself in the house of Rimmon.

¹⁹ And he said unto him, Go in peace. So he departed from him a little way.

A third tremendously important characteristic of the ministry of Elisha is that he isn't religious. Elisha discerned that Naaman's heart was right and sent him forth in peace without trying to force him through a bunch of religious hoops. Jesus' teaching doesn't center on religious practice or rituals either, but rather on the heart.

Elisha didn't threaten Naaman by saying it would be the end of the world (or of his healing) if he were to enter the house of Rimmon with his master. God revealed to Elisha that Naaman no longer had a heart to worship Rimmon. His position required that he must go there out of proper respect for his master, but his heart was no longer in it. This is what is most important to God. So Elisha told him to go in peace.

²⁰ But Gehazi, the servant of Elisha the man of God, said, Behold, my master has spared Naaman, this Syrian, in not receiving at his hands that which he brought. As the LORD lives, I will run after him and take something from him.

Signs in previous verses revealed Gehazi didn't have the same heart for God as Elisha. Gehazi, though very gifted, didn't have the capacity to hear directly from the LORD or to see into the spiritual realm. Gehazi means "contemplated pride."

Like many today, Gehazi thought Elisha had prevented Naaman from receiving an even greater blessing from God by not taking the money Naaman offered. Gehazi couldn't bear to see Naaman leave with the money. He even swore an oath by the LORD that he would take some of it from him. Much of this goes on almost everywhere today. Sooner or later everyone will be tried and tested.

I have seen or known of cases when some important pagan was brought to repentance by the power of God. Then the pastor or evangelist piles on the guilt and takes his gold watch or gold ring or some of the other things he has. Some even take the expensive paintings on the wall and the TV by saying these things have been compromised by the devil and must be surrendered to the pastor in order for the person to come out from under a curse and be blessed.

When someone is touched by the power of God, they are vulnerable, and we must be careful to only do and say what God decrees. Jesus told the rich, young ruler to go and sell all of his (possibly ill-gotten) riches and give all the money to the poor — then to come and follow him. Jesus made it clear that it was the young man who was valuable to him. Scripture states that Jesus loved him, and it is clear he wasn't interested in obtaining any of his earthly possessions (Matthew 19:16).

> 21 So Gehazi followed after Naaman. And when Naaman saw him running after him, he lighted down from the chariot to meet him and said, Is there no peace?
>
> 22 And he said, Peace. My master has sent me, saying, Behold, even now two young men of the sons of the prophets came to me from Mount Ephraim; give them, I pray thee, a talent of silver and two changes of garments.
>
> 23 And Naaman said, If you wish take two talents. And he urged him and bound two talents of silver in two bags with two changes of garments and laid them upon two of his servants; and they bore them before him.
>
> 24 And when he came to a secret place, he took them from their hand and bestowed them in the house; and he let the men go, and they departed.

In the holy place of the temple, a veil shielded the priests from the direct presence of God. This is being done away with. Radical changes are presently underway. In the recent past servants of God could be involved in serious shenanigans, and it might take quite a while to expose that what they're doing isn't pleasing to God. Not anymore. In the dawning day of the LORD, the true ministers of the LORD will stand in the holy of holies in the presence of God. This is symbolically where Elijah and Elisha stood and where we will stand, if we minister unto the LORD in the new day.

> 25 But when he went in and stood before his master, Elisha said unto him, From where comest thou, Gehazi? And he said, Thy servant went nowhere.
>
> 26 Then he said unto him, Did not my heart go with thee when the man turned again from his chariot to meet thee? Is it a time to receive money and to receive garments and oliveyards and vineyards and sheep and oxen and menslaves and maidslaves?
>
> 27 The leprosy therefore of Naaman shall cleave unto thee and unto thy seed for ever. And he went out from his presence a leper as white as snow.

There are also ministers today like Gehazi who love the things of this world more than they love God. The life of Adam, the life of the flesh, hasn't been circumcised from their hearts even though they may operate in gifts and ministries from God. Elisha's heart went with Gehazi, and he was dismayed. Those who feed and nurture the life of Adam will never be free from sin. The leprosy of Naaman will affect their seed forever.

We are headed into a special time in God, where the Lord will bless his people as never before. Countless Christians teach and/or have been taught the millennium is a time when we will live like kings, taking and doing whatever we please. According to Elisha, this isn't the case; even in the time of victory in the Lord, we aren't to twist arms or seek to take money, things, or even people to ourselves. We must remain content with what God gives us. Why would he mention such things as olive gardens, vineyards, sheep and oxen, and male and female slaves in addition to money and garments, if this wasn't a message for us?

The special time that is at hand is a time when the fear of the Lord will be restored. The Word of God will also be restored upon the earth, and it shall be clear who the true representatives of the Lord really are.

Until this point, Gehazi could serve and minister under the prophet Elisha. With leprosy, however, he had to live apart. If he walked down the streets of any city or town, he was required to cry, "Unclean, unclean," in order to warn people, so they wouldn't catch his contagious, incurable disease.

Gehazi had served Elisha for so long, he'd witnessed the resurrection of the son of the family that had helped Elisha. After seeing numerous miracles from God, when Gehazi finally showed what was in his heart, Elisha didn't say, "Look, Gehazi, repent, I will give you one last chance. Go and return the money and the garments you accepted from Naaman."

No! When Gehazi did what he did, Elisha didn't take the things away from him. Gehazi was allowed to keep them, but he also kept the leprosy of Naaman upon him and upon his seed forever. Gehazi wasn't given a second chance. He was immediately disqualified from the realm of the holy of holies, from the realm of ministry unto the LORD.

The prophet Ezekiel prophesied this same type of thing. The priesthood (now the priesthood of all believers) will be divided. Priests who taught Israel to sin will be denied access to the presence of God. They will be allowed to minister outside — butchering the "flesh" of the "sacrifices" and doing menial tasks. Only the priests from the line of Zadoc, meaning "righteousness and justice," will be allowed to minister in the presence of God and go back and forth between God and the people like Elisha (Ezekiel 44:10-16).

Leprosy is a symbol of serious sin that must be quarantined. Under normal conditions, it can't be reversed, but God can heal and forgive. In the case of Naaman, the Lord healed him. In the case of Gehazi, nothing more could be done. In the very face of the victorious ministry of Elisha, Gehazi didn't believe in victory and obviously didn't live in victory. In view of this, how could he ever conduct others into victory?

Those who live defeated lives tend to think or convince themselves that everyone else is just like them and are ready to make the person aware of their sin and guilt. Instead of pointing them to victory in Christ, they offer to absolve them with religious ritual and therapy. In other words, they use defeat to strengthen their own kingdoms, because under this type of ministry, people continue to sin, and the ministers continue infusing guilt and teaching there is no lasting victory.

The victory isn't in us; it is in the Lord Jesus Christ, and he's not seeking to become victorious. He already is. In the same way, he isn't seeking cleanness. He's already clean and victorious, and he desires to come and reign from our hearts. His desire is to transform our entire being. When this takes place, it isn't necessary to proselytize and recruit new adepts into the religious system of men. This is where the conflict lies.

Why did the king of Israel tear his clothes? Why was he upset by Naaman's request for healing and victory? It's because the king knew the prophet Elisha existed. He'd seen and heard of the mighty works of God. Even so, it didn't even occur to the king to send Naaman to see Elisha. Instead, the Spirit of God revealed the situation to Elisha who then sent word to Naaman. It was God who was finally able to deal with Naaman.

The Lord isn't trying to save the old man. He seeks the death of the old man, so we may emerge in the new man in Christ. In order for this to happen, each person must receive revelation from God. Participation in religious ritual isn't enough. This is why Elijah sent Naaman to the Jordan.

When Naaman told Elisha, *From now on thy slave will offer neither burnt offering nor sacrifice unto other gods, but unto the LORD.* This was all it took. His response satisfied God, and Elisha told him to go in peace, even if on occasion he might have to accompany his master into the house of Rimmon.

On judgment day, it will be fascinating to see what God does with each and every individual. I am sure Naaman, the Syrian general, will enter into life while I fear this may not be the case for many kings of "Israel" and even kings of "Judah."

A moment in history is approaching when those who demonstrate the attitude of Gehazi may find they have gone beyond a point of no return and no longer have the possibility to rectify the condition of their hearts.

Gehazi isn't the only example in Scripture. Judas might have come to repentance, except that he showed up at the Last Supper with thirty pieces of silver in his pocket — silver paid to him to betray the Lord. Even afterward, when he attempted to repent, it was too late, and as a result he committed suicide and never made it to the resurrection.

Remember the story of Ananias and Sapphira? In the midst of miraculous deeds performed by God early in the book of Acts, Peter didn't confront them and give them a chance to rectify themselves. No! They lied to the Holy Spirit and fell over dead.

Leprosy leads to death, just as advanced sin leads to spiritual death. This is what happened in the life of Gehazi. Flaws in his character and heart weren't rectified at the proper time and became irreversible. Finally God pronounced sentence through Elisha.

What will happen to those in ministry who have clearly demonstrated a desire for the things of this world above and beyond the will and the Word of God? What will happen to those who use their God-given gifts and ministry for personal gain?

God grants opportunity, a lot of opportunity, for a time in which repentance is readily available. However, there is also a time when God closes the door to repentance. This is what happened to the devil and his angels. Scripture states that repentance wasn't granted to them.

Why? Because they rebelled against God with their eyes wide open. They knew and experienced the glory of God. Therefore, it wasn't possible to bring them to repentance by demonstrating the grace and glory of God to them. There wasn't anything else that could be revealed to them about God that would cause them to change their mind.

This differs from the case of Naaman who was completely bowled over by the love, mercy, and grace of God, when he was healed of his incurable disease. I am sure he remained grateful and thankful for the rest of his life. Jesus even mentioned Naaman as an example (Luke 4:27).

In numerous places, the church doesn't display sufficient fear of the Lord. Countless people think the Lord will persist in giving them opportunity after opportunity after opportunity. And it is true that the Lord gives a great deal of opportunity to repent and to draw near to him. It isn't true, however, that the opportunity is limitless. Think of how God dealt with Pharaoh. Sooner or later, a cutoff point will be reached.

This cutoff point will occur when the Lord decides to put certain things in their proper place or perspective. One of these things is his desire to have a people willing to represent him as he really is. As in the day of Elisha, corrupt governments may continue for a while, but God desires a clean ministry, and he will soon separate those who minister with clean hearts like Elisha from those with corrupt hearts like Gehazi.

Many don't understand the book of 2 Kings. The kings come to an end. The ten tribes of Israel come to an end. Judah is taken into captivity. The world as we know it will come to an end, but the ministry of God won't end. True ministry is placed by God. And the clean Word of God which flows through those God chooses won't come to an end. God is no respecter of persons. The little, seemingly insignificant slave girl was greatly used by God.

Why did Naaman believe her word? Her life was an inspiring example. The commanding general of the Syrian army believed in her word to the point that he was willing to go on a long journey into Israel to seek healing and salvation.

The only requirement necessary to being used effectively by God is to have a clean heart. A person with a clean heart cannot be hidden. They will be noticed.

We are entering into a time of numerous changes. The people of God will know victory, but victory in the eyes of God doesn't necessarily equate to taking over the White House, the Presidential Palace, or even the Vatican. It may have nothing to do with taking hold of the reins of governments of this world. All the kingdoms of this world will be brought down, and God's kingdom will visibly rise when the seventh trumpet sounds (Revelation 11:15).

Even when the children of Israel entered into the Promised Land, they didn't really take anything by their own might. The Lord gave them houses they didn't build, wells they hadn't dug, and vineyards and olive groves they didn't plant. God displaced the previous corrupt owners and gave his people their inheritance.

The problem with Gehazi was that he decided to take things into his own hands. When God isn't the one giving something to us, it's terrible to take it for ourselves, even from an enemy.

Scripture states that when we walk in victory with the Lord, the blessing will come up from behind and overtake us (Deuteronomy 28:2).

### Let us pray:

Heavenly Father, may we learn this important lesson before it is too late. May we understand the problem of Gehazi and your dealings with Naaman and with the king of Israel.

We ask, Lord that we may be content with whatever you see fit to give us and with whatever place and situation where you have placed us. We ask this in the name of the Lord Jesus Christ. Amen.

# Chapter Twelve
## Seeing from God's Perspective

### 2 Kings 6

¹ The sons of the prophets said unto Elisha, Behold now, the place where we dwell with thee is too tight for us.

At the time of the prophet Elijah, he was the only true prophet among hundreds of false prophets. We have come through a time like this in which the only true prophet is our Lord Jesus Christ, who acts through those who are clean, while countless false prophets are also mingled among the people of God.

As described here in 2 Kings, a change in the prophetic ministry takes place even before Elisha came into the double portion. A large company of "sons of the prophets" lived in community in close relationship with one another. This foreshadowed what took place in the early church after the day of pentecost, and I believe this practice will revive under a double-portion anointing in the very near future.

The plan of God is to have a body of Christ made up of many members. Each member is to have a direct connection to the head of the body and is to be nourished and bonded with the other members of the body (Ephesians 4:15-16). Therefore, if we are in a right relationship with Jesus, the head, he will automatically bring us into relationship with everyone else who is right with him. This is how the true temple of God (made of living stones) will come together without the sound of a hammer or iron tool (1 Kings 6:7).

We are heading into this change in the history of the church because the Lord Jesus is the example for all of us; it is his desire that we be like him and together we all go on to even greater things (John 14:12). Greater things? Why? How? More people will be clean and, as a result, God will be able to work through his body without limitation.

> Behold now, the place where we dwell with thee is too tight for us. (v. 1)

This isn't like when they had a separate "school" of the prophets. At this point they all lived with Elisha, which means "God of the coming (one)."

> ² Let us go, we pray thee, unto the Jordan, and each one take a beam from there, and let us make us a place there where we may dwell. And he answered, Go.
> ³ And one said, Be content, I pray thee, and go with thy slaves. And he answered, I will go.
> ⁴ So he went with them. And when they came to the Jordan, they cut down the wood.
> ⁵ But as one was felling a beam, the axe head fell into the water, and he cried and said, Alas, master! It was borrowed.
> ⁶ And the man of God said, Where did it fall? And he showed him the place. Then he cut down a stick and cast it in there and caused the iron to swim.
> ⁷ And he said unto him, Take it. And he put out his hand and took it.

Iron is a symbol of law. The iron axe head was borrowed.

When Solomon's temple was put together, no iron tools were used. This immense building was built without the sound of a hammer at the construction site. Those who choose to "borrow" the law of the past are unaware that it is destined to sink. This includes those who desire to place Christians back under the law (or under their own version of law). All this will sink. It is borrowed from the past.

The stick Elisha cast into the river to make the iron float to the surface represents the way of the cross. The way of the cross is the way of death to our own life, so the life of Jesus may shine through us. This is the way of mercy and grace that reverses the effects of the law. The law of sin and death was unable to hold the Lord Jesus Christ. He rose from the dead and with his release from death came a new law of the Spirit of life (Romans 8:2). This is the path we are to follow. This is what causes the borrowed iron axe head to float.

Countless Christian groups, organizations, and denominations still hold on to a long list of external governing laws. Some of them require members to sign statements saying they won't smoke, drink, dance, or do this or not do that. Some require a certain dress code or conduct. No matter what they insist on, even if they require their women to cover themselves from their head to their ankles, it won't ensure holiness. In fact, it won't really guarantee anything, because these types of external governance won't fix a corrupt heart. In contrast, those governed by the Holy Spirit have clean, pure hearts and will, by the very nature of the life of God within them, have chaste, moderate, clean behavior.

## Slaves to Sin Versus Those Free in Christ

> 8 Then the king of Syria warred against Israel and took counsel with his slaves, saying, In such and such a place shall be my camp.
>
> 9 And the man of God sent unto the king of Israel, saying, Beware not to pass through such and such a place, for the Syrians are going there.
>
> 10 Then the king of Israel sent to the place, which the man of God told him and warned him of and kept himself from there, not once nor twice.

To sum this up. Israel was at war with Syria, and the king of Syria kept attempting to ambush Israel. Each time this happened, Elisha warned the king of Israel of the location of the ambush so they wouldn't pass that way.

Remember that the king of Israel (the king of the people of God) wasn't really a good king. He controlled the people of God according to the ways of men. This king married the daughter of Jezebel who had mixed the things of God with the worship of Baal (the god of control and prosperity). Baal means "husband or master or controller."

This king was like many pastors, priests, and religious leaders today, who have mixed the worship of God with the worldly religious way of doing things. Therefore, they are married to the wrong system. The king thought he was the controller of everyone. Even so, Elisha helped the people of God see God's true plan, so they would understand and repent.

> [11] Therefore, the heart of the king of Syria was sore troubled over this thing, and he called his slaves and said unto them, Will ye not show me which of us is for the king of Israel?

He thought they had a spy in their midst.

> [12] Then one of his slaves said, None, my lord, O king, but Elisha, the prophet that is in Israel, tells the king of Israel the words that thou speakest in thy bedchamber.

Why was this happening? God was setting the stage for the time of the end. He poured out mercy and grace upon his people in the hope they would wholeheartedly turn to him. He gave the wicked king of Israel, those of the house of Ahab and the worshippers of Baal, their final opportunities to witness the character of God. Instead of having a mixed multitude of wheat and tares growing together in the same field, the tares would soon be taken out from among the wheat. The wicked would be removed from among the righteous. Things wouldn't continue as they had always been.

> [13] And he said, Go and spy where he is, that I may send and take him. And it was told him, saying, Behold, he is in Dothan.

Dothan means "two wells."

> [14] So he sent horsemen and chariots there and a great host, who came by night and compassed the city about.
>
> [15] And when the servant of the man of God was risen early to go forth, behold, a host compassed the city both with horsemen and chariots. And his servant said unto him, Alas, my master! What shall we do?

The servant of the man of God was no longer Gehazi, for he was afflicted with leprosy for the rest of his life. A new servant came on the scene, and God was about to reveal something to this servant — something he couldn't reveal to Gehazi.

May the LORD open our eyes to see what is really going on in the spiritual realm — that we'd see by the Spirit and become aware of the fiery chariots and horsemen of the heavenly hosts standing all around us, outnumbering our enemies and ready to go into action.

> [16] And he answered, Fear not; for those that are with us are more than those that are with them.
>
> [17] And Elisha prayed and said, LORD, I pray thee, open his eyes, that he may see. And the LORD opened the eyes of the young man, and he saw, and, behold, the mountain was full of horsemen and chariots of fire round about Elisha.

A chariot of fire with horses of fire had separated Elijah from Elisha. Then horsemen and chariots of fire surrounded Elisha, so the enemy couldn't touch him. This is the second time that Elisha had come into very close contact with the fire of God. His previous servant had become a leper for life, something that would affect all of Gehazi's descendants forever. In the new day, God separated the tares from among the wheat. Elisha's new young servant had a pure heart and Jesus said, *Blessed are the pure in heart, for they shall see God* (Matthew 5:8).

God opens the eyes of those with a pure heart. The young man was able to perceive the situation from God's point of view. If we keep our eyes on the world (even on the religious world) and on those who desire to harm us, we won't see what God is doing or what he desires to do.

> [18] And when the Syrians came down to him, Elisha prayed unto the LORD and said, Smite these people, I pray thee, with blindness. And he smote them with blindness according to the word of Elisha.

Elisha didn't attempt to give orders to the horsemen and chariots of fire. We aren't to give orders to the angels of God. We aren't to pray to the saints who have gone before us. Our communion is directly with the Lord, and he is the one who manages his heavenly hosts.

The LORD smote the enemy with blindness according to the word of Elisha.

> ¹⁹ And Elisha said unto them, This is not the way, neither is this the city; follow me, and I will bring you to the man whom ye seek. And he led them to Samaria.
>
> ²⁰ And when they came into Samaria, Elisha said, LORD, open the eyes of these men, that they may see. And the LORD opened their eyes, and they saw; and, behold, they were in the midst of Samaria.

Samaria wasn't doing all that well with the Lord. They had invented their own feast, instead of keeping the Feast of Tabernacles. They still worshipped golden calves and made priests of common people who weren't from the line of Aaron. Even with all this going on, however, a faithful remnant still existed. Therefore, God still offered help and salvation to his faithful remnant and waited to see if the others would return wholeheartedly unto him.

> ²¹ And the king of Israel said unto Elisha, when he saw them, My father, shall I smite them? Shall I smite them?

At this point the king of Israel was ready to receive orders from Elisha!

> ²² And he answered, Thou shalt not smite them; would thou smite those whom thou hast taken captive with thy sword and with thy bow? Set bread and water before them, that they may eat and drink and return to their master.

Jesus said we are to feed our enemies if they are hungry, and we are to give them something to drink if they are thirsty. We are to overcome evil with good.

> ²³ And he prepared great provision for them; and when they had eaten and drunk, he sent them away, and they went to their master. So the bands of Syria came no more into the land of Israel.

It looked like everything was on track to a happy conclusion, but sadly this wasn't the case. The kings hadn't learned the lesson. The bands of Syria didn't come back and plunder Israel, but the king of Israel and the king of Syria didn't learn the lesson God desired to teach them, although I'm sure many on both sides perceived what God was doing. Those with pure hearts like Elisha's new servant and maybe those in both armies who had or who desired to have pure hearts were undoubtedly amazed at the outstanding and unprecedented events that took place.

Many today are like those ancient kings. We all have the God-given ability to make choices and decisions that have the possibility of affecting our own lives as well as making an impact on the lives of others. Yet many, even after repeatedly experiencing the grace and goodness and miracles of God, don't really learn the lesson.

## The Stubbornness of the King Prevails

> 24 And it came to pass after this, that Benhadad, king of Syria, gathered all his host and went up and besieged Samaria.

Remember that King Ahab had the opportunity to do away with Benhadad once and for all, but he forfeited that golden opportunity by making him an ally; he wanted to provide what he thought would be ongoing safety and freedom for the people of Israel while sharing the evil power of his enemy. The bottom line is that he didn't listen to the LORD.

Large sectors of the church have done something similar. They've made peace with the natural man. They've missed opportunity after opportunity to put to death the deeds of the flesh by the Spirit. Even though they've been warned, they still don't believe what God says.

> For if ye live according to the flesh, ye shall die; but if through the Spirit ye mortify the deeds of the body, ye shall live. (Romans 8:13)

Those who continue to fraternize with Jezebel and her false prophets will come into great tribulation (Revelation 2:20-23).

> ²⁵ And there was a great famine in Samaria as they besieged it until an ass's head was sold for eighty pieces of silver and the fourth part of a cab of dove's dung for five pieces of silver.

This was significant. Things began to move rapidly from bad to worse (Deuteronomy 28:15-68).

> ²⁶ And as the king of Israel was passing by upon the wall, a woman cried unto him, saying, Save me, my lord, O king.
>
> ²⁷ And he said, If the LORD does not save thee, from where shall I save thee? Out of the threshing floor, or out of the winepress?
>
> ²⁸ And the king said unto her, What ails thee? And she answered, This woman said unto me, Give thy son that we may eat him today, and we will eat my son tomorrow.
>
> ²⁹ So we boiled my son and ate him. And I said unto her on the next day, Give thy son that we may eat him. But she has hid her son.
>
> ³⁰ And when the king heard the words of the woman, he rent his clothes; and he passed by like this upon the wall, and the people looked, and, behold, he had sackcloth within upon his flesh.

The king put on sackcloth underneath his royal robes, which represented repentance, because he didn't want to repent publicly, even when terrible abominations were occurring right in his face.

Leaders of Christian organizations today are in more and more trouble similar to that of the king of Israel. They know God is beginning to judge their situation. Things that have no other explanation are taking place, and while they've put on sackcloth, it is beneath their royal robes.

In private, they cry out to the Lord asking him to get them out of their ever-increasing trouble. In public, however, they don't want to admit to having built their own kingdoms. They don't want to publicly repent of their collective, corporate sins. They refuse to acknowledge that they've built powerful religious machines that not only take away the liberty of the people of God but also block the people from being freely led by the Holy Spirit. They have used the false prophets of Jezebel to control the people.

Now the king of Israel was about to do something even worse.

> 31 Then he said, God do so and more also to me, if the head of Elisha, the son of Shaphat, shall remain on him today.

Instead of taking responsibility and leading the people into genuine and open repentance, the king of Israel blamed Elisha for all of his problems. Why? Because Elisha had captured his enemies but didn't allow him to kill them. Then, in the midst of great tribulation, the king decided to kill Elisha despite the fact that it was his own father, Ahab, who spared enemy king Benhadad who is now causing him all the damage!

When Jezebel threatened to kill Elijah, he ran. When the king threatened to kill Elisha, he didn't run.

> 32 And Elisha sat in his house, and the elders sat with him; and the king sent a man unto him. But before the messenger came to him, he said to the elders, See ye how this son of a murderer has sent to take away my head? Look, when the messenger comes, shut the door, and hold him fast at the door, is not the sound of his master's feet behind him?

They were coming to kill him, and Elisha sat there patiently with the elders.

> 33 And while he yet talked with them, behold, the messenger came down unto him; and he said, Behold, this evil is of the LORD; for what should I wait for the LORD any longer?

They didn't only blame Elisha; they also blamed all of their misfortune on the LORD.

Jesus mused, *When the son of man returns, will he find faith upon the earth?* Prophetically, the earth is the realm of Israel and the church.

Elisha was a representation of the Lord, and he didn't find faith in the king or in many of the people of Israel (the people of God). Yet a faithful remnant of seven thousand remained who hadn't bowed their knee to Baal. Among the sons of the prophets, there was a faithful group; a number of people, including the elders, continued to listen to Elisha. The word *elder* in Hebrew refers to maturity.

The Scriptures state that prior to the return of Jesus Christ, tribulation worse than any that has ever occurred will befall the earth, and if those days aren't shortened, no flesh will survive (Mark 13:20). During a period called the time of Jacob's trouble, many people of God will fear all is lost (Jeremiah 30:7). During that time, Scripture states that the love of many will grow cold.

**Let us pray:**

Heavenly Father, may we be found faithful until the end. May we always appreciate and give thanks for all you have done for us. May we always have hope, and may the fire of your love always burn brightly in our hearts.

May we remain standing upon the battlefield of life until your perfect will is accomplished in and through us. We ask this in the name of the Lord Jesus Christ. Amen.

# Chapter Thirteen

## The Tribulation is Unexpectedly Cut Short

### 2 Kings 7

¹ Then Elisha said, Hear ye the word of the LORD; Thus hath the LORD said, Tomorrow about this time a measure of fine flour shall be sold for a shekel and two measures of barley for a shekel, in the gate of Samaria.

² Then a captain on whose hand the king leaned answered the man of God and said, Behold, if the LORD would make windows in heaven, might this thing be? And he said, Behold, thou shalt see it with thine eyes, but shalt not eat of it.

This was likely the very same captain the king sent to cut off Elisha's head.

Four leprous men with nothing to lose:

³ And there were four leprous men at the entrance of the gate, who said one to another, Why shall we stay here until we die?

⁴ If we say, We will enter into the city, then the famine is in the city, and we shall die there; and if we stay here, we shall die also. Now therefore come, and let us fall unto the host of the Syrians; if they save us alive, we shall live; and if they kill us, we shall but die.

These four lepers played a crucial part in the plan of God.

⁵ And they rose up at the beginning of the night, to go unto the camp of the Syrians; and when they were come to the uttermost part of the camp of Syria, behold, there was no man there.

> ⁶ For the LORD had made the host of the Syrians to hear a noise of chariots and a noise of horses, even the noise of a great host; and they said one to another, Behold, the king of Israel has hired against us the kings of the Hittites and the kings of the Egyptians, to come upon us.
> ⁷ Therefore they had arisen and fled at the beginning of the night and had left their tents and their horses and their asses, even the camp as it was, and had fled for their lives.

What caused the noise of chariots and horses heard by the Syrians? Consider this. The host of the LORD surrounded the city of Dothan when the Syrians planned to trap and kill Elisha, and the LORD opened the eyes of the young servant of Elisha, so he could see things from God's point of view. This same heavenly host must have continued to support Elisha and the faithful remnant — those who didn't bend their knee to Baal. God never abandons his own. When God sends judgment, he never destroys the righteous along with the wicked. (Genesis 18:23-33)

> ⁸ And when these lepers came to the uttermost part of the camp, they went into one tent and ate and drank and took silver and gold and raiment and went and hid it and came again and entered into another tent and took from there also and went and hid it.

Four lepers raided the enemy camp and enjoyed a feast while the rest of the people of God were dying of starvation inside the city of religion.

> ⁹ Then they said one to another, We do not well; this day is a day to give good tidings, and we are silent; if we tarry until the morning light, we shall be taken in the iniquity. Now, therefore, come, that we may enter in and give the news in the king's house.

The four lepers still had a conscience. Iniquity is when a person does the wrong thing, knowing full well what they are doing is wrong.

¹⁰ So they came and called unto the porter of the city, and they told them, saying, We went to the camp of the Syrians, and, behold, there was no man there, neither voice of man, but horses tied and asses tied, and the tents as they were.

¹¹ And the porters cried out and told it inside and in the king's house.

¹² And the king arose in the night and said unto his slaves, I will now show you what the Syrians have done to us. They know that we are hungry; therefore, they have gone out of the camp to hide themselves in the field, saying, When they come out of the city, we shall catch them alive and get into the city.

The king was incapable of receiving good news (the gospel is good news). He couldn't believe it when God sent a message through the prophet Elisha that there would be deliverance and salvation by morning. On top of that, he couldn't believe the four lepers. The conscience and discernment of the four lepers proved much better than that of the king.

¹³ Then one of his slaves answered and said, Let some take, I pray thee, five of the horses that remain, which are left in the city (for they are as all the multitude of Israel that are left in it; they are also as all the multitude of the Israelites that are consumed) and let us send and see.

¹⁴ They took, therefore, two chariot horses; and the king sent after the camp of the Syrians, saying, Go and see.

¹⁵ And they went after them unto the Jordan; and, behold, all the way was full of garments and vessels, which the Syrians had cast away in their haste. And the messengers returned and told the king.

¹⁶ Then the people went out and spoiled the camp of the Syrians. So a measure of fine flour was sold for a shekel and two measures of barley for a shekel, according to the word of the LORD.

¹⁷ And the king appointed the prince on whose hand he leaned to have the charge of the gate; and the people trode

upon him in the gate, and he died, as the man of God had said, who spoke when the king came down to him.

¹⁸ And it came to pass as the man of God had spoken to the king, saying, Two measures of barley for a shekel, and a measure of fine flour for a shekel shall be tomorrow about this time in the gate of Samaria.

¹⁹ Unto which that prince had answered the man of God, and said, Even if the LORD should make windows in heaven, might such a thing be? And he said, Behold, thou shalt see it with thine eyes, but shalt not eat of it.

²⁰ And so it happened unto him, for the people trode upon him in the gate, and he died.

There comes a time when the person who has refused to hear the Word of the Lord will no longer have another opportunity. It will be too late.

On that day when people of the city enjoyed the spoils of the Syrian camp, most of them had another chance, but not that captain. In this realm, he was a man of authority and power, the right-hand man to the king. He had the ear of the king. In fact, he even gave him bad advice. As the people rushed out of the city to plunder the Syrian camp, this captain thought he was in control, but he had used up his last opportunity.

The time is coming when many of those who have controlled things (and who have helped others to control) will have their last chance. Others who haven't had much of a chance will have their opportunity. For example, when Gehazi took the things from Naaman, he kept them, but he also got Naaman's leprosy. In contrast, when God sent deliverance and blessing to his people in the city, the four lepers who were outside the city were the first to receive it. Isn't this interesting?

Gehazi not only accepted the things of Naaman, but he also hid the money and clothing in a secret place and pretended he hadn't gone anywhere. In the case of the four lepers, they were reminded by their conscience that they should immediately let the king and the city know the wonderful news of what the LORD had done.

When the Lord provides for us, it's much, much different from when we attempt to take matters into our own hands. We aren't authorized to control and manipulate things. The Scripture states that *Man shall not live by bread alone, but by every word that proceeds out of the mouth of God.*

The days in which it was possible to build a religious fortress, according to the ways of men, are coming to an end. That which will survive and endure, surging forth in the authority of the Lord, is a people in which each person has his own link to the Lord.

We can learn several important things about Elisha in this narrative:

- Elisha didn't grandstand or foment a personality cult around himself. He didn't attempt to personally control the other prophets; he focused on giving the Word of the LORD. Each prophet was under the direct control of the LORD, and therefore each one respected the authority that God had placed upon Elisha.
- Elisha didn't ever have to hide or run. Unlike Elijah who ran from Jezebel and was very ashamed afterward, Elisha never ran from trouble in his entire ministry.

The world system and the religious system couldn't overcome him. The Word of the Lord through Elisha was always true and remained firm. In the dawn of the new day, the Lord will have a people like this.

**Let us pray:**

Heavenly Father, we thank you for the example of Elisha. May we take this to heart and trust you fully. We ask this in the name of our Lord Jesus Christ. Amen.

# Chapter Fourteen
## A Spiritual Famine

Along with the double portion ministry of Elisha came more responsibility for the kings and people. Paul preached that in the times of ignorance, God overlooked (or winked at) many things, but with the preaching of the gospel, God was commanding all men everywhere to repent (Acts 17:30). Scripture also states that to whom much is given, much will be required (Luke 12:48).

Those who don't really desire to hear the Word of God and choose not to respond to the voice of God, refusing to bow before the sovereignty of God, will never learn to be led by the Spirit of God. These people are condemned to wander in a zig-zag between legalism and licentiousness until time runs out for them. Often, if parents are very legalistic, the children lunge towards licentiousness or vice versa.

### 2 Kings 8

> ¹ Then Elisha spoke unto the woman, whose son he had restored to life, saying, Arise, and go thou and thine household and sojourn wherever thou canst sojourn; for the LORD has called for a famine which shall come upon the land seven years.

When Elijah stood before evil King Ahab, he announced there would be no more rain. How long was the drought? Jesus said it lasted three years and six months (Luke 4:25).

The double portion ministry became much clearer, accompanied with abundant undeniable evidence of miracles, blessing, and sovereignty of God; yet when the mercy of God is rejected, the ensuing drought is also double.

If King Ahab struggled to find a little grass to keep some of his horses and mules alive at the end of three and a half years of drought (to sustain his walk in the flesh), what will happen after seven years of drought? For us, it will ensure that no one will be able to stay alive spiritually, unless they surrender their walk in the flesh, their private kingdoms, and even their own lives to the Lord. This is the same picture as what happened with Joseph in Egypt when the people were forced to sell their livestock first, then their lands, and finally themselves to Joseph in order to stay alive (Genesis 47:13-26).

Remember that a woman often represents an entire group of people in Scripture. This drought promised to be so bad that the woman and her household were warned by Elisha to leave Israel and go elsewhere. Anywhere else would be better.

In churches today, a drought for the true Word of the Lord has many families, leaving so they don't starve to death spiritually. Those leaving established churches don't even know exactly where they're going. The only clear instructions they have from the Lord are that they must leave "Israel" until the "seven years" of drought are over.

> [2] Then the woman arose and did as the man of God told her; and she went with her household and sojourned in the land of the Philistines seven years.

The land of the Philistines is the land of death, the land of secular enemies. When God prepared David and his mighty men to deliver Israel, they also were sent to live in the land of the Philistines. In fact, many Philistines became loyal to David and came to be part of David's victorious men.

> [3] And it came to pass at the end of the seven years that the woman returned out of the land of the Philistines, and she went forth to cry unto the king for her house and for her lands.
>
> [4] And the king had talked with Gehazi, the servant of the man of God, saying, Tell me, I pray thee, all the great things that Elisha has done.

Remember Gehazi? As I mentioned earlier, his name means "contemplation of pride." He became a lifelong leper, because he sought personal gain when Naaman, the enemy general, was healed of leprosy.

Even after seven years of famine, Gehazi and the king didn't cry out to God for mercy because they were already dead in trespasses and sin. God had foretold of the famine as an opportunity for them to repent, but they weren't repentant. Instead, they sat around telling stories of the good old days when God did miracles through the hand of Elisha.

This is like dead churches today, where no real spiritual food has been served for quite some time. Yet those attending still sit around telling stories about miracles from church history's past and things written in the Bible. Never mind that great things of God aren't happening in their midst today.

Some teach that we live in a time of the silence of God today. Others have witnessed so many false prophets and false miracle workers that they no longer believe. They are content to sit back and listen to stories of the early church, the Reformation, the Great Awakening, the Welsh Revival, Azuza Street, the 1948 Revival, or the 1967 Revival.

They sit like religious spectators in a backwards-looking rut where God isn't moving. They sit in their rebellion like the king of Israel and with the leprosy of their sin like Gehazi, instead of falling on their faces to seek the Lord.

> [5] And as he was telling the king how he had restored a dead body to life, behold, the woman, whose son he had restored to life, cried to the king for her house and for her land. So Gehazi said, My lord, O king, this is the woman, and this is her son, whom Elisha restored to life.

The Lord does things like this. When people are complacent, he may leave things alone until the time is right for him to send his Word and testimony once again. After seven years of famine, he sent the very same woman, along with the very same son who had been raised from the dead, to stand before the king.

> [6] And when the king asked the woman, she told him. Then the king appointed unto her a eunuch, saying, Restore all

that was hers and all the fruits of the lands since the day that she left the lands, even until now.

What do you think about this? God sent the woman away from Israel during the seven years of "famine," and when she returned, she hadn't lost a single thing. The evil king of Israel gave back her lands and all the fruits of it during the seven years! We have other examples of God working like this, beginning with Joseph in Egypt when they experienced seven years of plenty followed by seven years of famine.

All of this ties into the prophecy and orders given to Elijah in 1 Kings 19 after the fire fell from heaven and the killing of all the prophets of Baal at the time when Elijah ran away from Jezebel to the mountain of God to protect his life.

God took Elijah on a long path toward victory. Elisha had to accompany Elijah through some dealings with God at the Jordan River, where he surrendered his life and was caught up victorious into eternity. Not only this, but Elijah left Elisha a victorious mantle and sowed the seeds for a victorious overcoming company of sons of the prophets who lived to see the demise of Jezebel and of all the worshippers of Baal. After receiving this mantle, Elisha never ran and he never complained. He followed and learned from the example of Elijah and walked in perfect victory. Elisha was called by God to follow up and complete those things Elijah hadn't finished. Do you remember what they were?

Here is a reminder of what the LORD had said to Elijah:

> And the LORD said unto him, Go, return on thy way by the wilderness of Damascus; and thou shalt arrive there and anoint Hazael to be king of Syria; and Jehu, the son of Nimshi, thou shalt anoint to be king over Israel; and Elisha, the son of Shaphat of Abelmeholah, thou shalt anoint to be prophet in thy place.
>
> And it shall be that he that escapes the sword of Hazael, Jehu shall slay; and he that escapes from the sword of Jehu, Elisha shall slay. And I will cause seven thousand to remain in Israel, all the knees which have not bowed

unto Baal, and every mouth which has not kissed him.
(1 Kings 19:15-18)

(At the time these instructions were given by God directly to Elijah, Hazael and Jehu were young boys, and Elisha was about thirty. It would take another twenty-five years for all of this to be accomplished.)

Faulty translations have created a misunderstanding regarding this passage. What God was really saying here is that the Lord is going to root the tares out of the people of God, and in the midst of judgment, he will cause seven thousand righteous persons to remain who aren't tainted in any way with Baal. Prophetically, seven thousand means the perfect number of all those who are truly redeemed. The people of God (Israel and the church) are about to go through the judgment of God, and God promises that "seven thousand" will remain. This judgment will come from three sides, symbolized by Hazael, Jehu, and Elisha (who all have their respective friends and allies).

When God first gave this word to Elijah, it seemed it would be implemented immediately. This, however, wasn't the case. The only thing that happened more or less immediately was the calling of Elisha (who wasn't anointed with the double portion until years later). It was more than twenty-five years after the call of Elisha and several years after Elijah was taken home to glory that the remainder of the instructions God gave Elijah were about to be fulfilled.

In recent history, similar things happened decades ago and are happening today. I'm convinced we'll soon see the fulfillment of things promised years ago. After all of the drought we've experienced, God wants us to remember that man does not *live by bread alone, but by every word that proceeds out of the mouth of God.*

The church in Colombia, the church in the United States, in fact the church all over the world (with a few exceptions like the land of the "Philistines") suffers from spiritual drought. And Gehazi has been telling the king (who can represent any of us who exercise any type of responsibility) the stories about what God did on a previous occasion. Countless churches and synagogues are full of various versions of the unrepentant king and Gehazi with his leprosy.

Elisha was clearly a continuation of the ministry of Elijah, just as Jesus followed the ministry of John the Baptist, who went in the spirit and power of Elijah. We are now coming into the time and season of the second coming of the Lord Jesus Christ. Remember, Elisha means "God of the coming (one)." Elisha is also repeatedly called "man of God." The Hebrew word here denotes a free born man instead of a slave. This is also a reference to the body of Christ, which is composed of those who are born again into freedom by the Spirit of God. For where the Spirit of the Lord is, there is liberty.

At the end of the "seven years" of drought, we are about to see a lot of action. God will once again send the rain of his blessing. He will send forth his Word, which is our spiritual sustenance. How will this come? Let's continue in 2 Kings 8 to see.

## 2 Kings 8

> ⁷ Elisha went to Damascus; and Ben-Hadad, the king of Syria, was sick; and it was told him, saying, The man of God is come here.

Normally someone important from Israel would think twice before walking into the city of the enemy for fear they'd be killed. Elisha, with his double portion anointing, went wherever God sent him. He stood firm and the enemy found themselves in trouble if they decided to mess with him.

> ⁸ And the king said unto Hazael, Take a present in thy hand, and go, meet the man of God and enquire of the LORD by him, saying, Shall I recover of this disease?

It seems the enemy king had more respect for Elisha than the king of Israel did. In fact, God used the Elisha ministry to touch and influence many among the enemies of Israel in Syria and elsewhere. This will also be the case today.

> ⁹ So Hazael went to meet him and took a present with him, even of every good thing of Damascus, forty camels' burden, and came and stood before him, and said, Thy son

Benhadad, king of Syria, has sent me to thee, saying, Shall I recover of this disease?

This wasn't a small "present."

<sup>10</sup> And Elisha said unto him, Go, say unto him, Thou may certainly recover. But the LORD has showed me that he shall surely die.

Look at this Word! Isn't this extremely interesting?

It was still possible for the king to recover. But the LORD showed Elisha that this definitely wouldn't be the case. Many prophetic words include this type of component, and last minute decisions and attitudes can still affect the outcome because God doesn't take away our free will. In this case, Hazael's intervention also put the final nail in the coffin for the king of Syria.

God knows the end from the beginning, but he still holds each and every one of us accountable for responsibilities he has placed in our hands.

This is a message for people today who act and feel like kings because they have responsibilities. Even so, it's still possible for them to come into spiritual health and salvation, but unfortunately, many of them will die in their sin and rebellion.

Elisha looked deeply into the eyes of Hazael, the enemy general.

<sup>11</sup> And he settled his countenance steadfastly, until he was ashamed; and the man of God wept.

<sup>12a</sup> Then Hazael said unto him, Why does my lord weep?

Elisha was remembering the Word of the LORD given to Elijah.

<sup>12b</sup> And he answered, Because I know the evil that thou wilt do unto the sons of Israel; their strong holds wilt thou set on fire, and their young men wilt thou slay with the sword and wilt dash their children and rip up their women with child.

God was about to use Hazael to effect judgment upon Israel. Everyone contaminated with Baal and who was unclean would be wiped out one way or another. Remember that Baal means "master, husband, or controller." Hazael means "whom God sees" or "whom God protects." God sees everyone, but God won't necessarily protect everyone.

Under certain conditions, the judgment of God can be postponed (1 Kings 21:29). Varying factors may cause God to delay judgment. God causes his sun of righteousness and his rain of blessing to come upon the just and the unjust.

A day of harvest — a day of reckoning — is certainly coming. When the fruit of the harvest isn't to God's liking, he will destroy it (Amos 8:1-3). This was about to happen to Israel, and God was going to use Hazael, who as we will see was ruthless. Many of God's people were confident God would never anoint their enemy to come against them. Elijah may have anointed Hazael years before according to the Word of the Lord. Now Elisha confirmed this Word.

> 13 And Hazael said, But what, is thy slave a dog, that he should do this great thing? And Elisha answered, The LORD has showed me that thou shalt be king over Syria.

Hazael, like many in Syria today, thought it a *great thing* to wipe out Israel. And remember that most who want to destroy Israel also desire to destroy the church.

> 14 So he departed from Elisha and came to his master; who said to him, What did Elisha say to thee? And he answered, He told me that thou may surely recover.
>
> 15 And it came to pass on the next day that he took a thick cloth and dipped it in water and spread it on his face so that he died; and Hazael reigned in his stead.

## At the Palace in Jerusalem

> 16 And in the fifth year of Joram, the son of Ahab, king of Israel, Jehoshaphat being then king of Judah, Jehoram, the son of Jehoshaphat king of Judah, began to reign.

Now we have two Jehorams; one was son of Ahab and Jezebel and the other was married to a daughter of Ahab and Jezebel. Jehoram means "whom the LORD has exalted." A lot of people in Israel and

Judah pretended that the LORD had exalted these two evil kings when in reality Jezebel and her minions were involved.

> [17] He was thirty-two years old when he began to reign, and he reigned eight years in Jerusalem.
>
> [18] He walked in the way of the kings of Israel, as did the house of Ahab, for the daughter of Ahab was his wife, and he did evil in the sight of the LORD.

As a result of the influence of Jezebel and the house of Ahab, things took a very bad turn in Judah.

> [19] Yet with all this, the LORD would not destroy Judah for David, his slave's sake, as he had promised him to give him always a light of his sons.

Due to the past heritage of godly men and women, the Lord hasn't completely withdrawn his presence (and protection) from many parts of the Christian church.

> [20] In his days, Edom revolted from under the hand of Judah and made a king over themselves.
>
> [21] So Joram went over to Zair and all his chariots with him, and he rose up by night and smote the Edomites, who had compassed him about, and the captains of the chariots; and the people fled into their tents.

Apparently Joram and Jehoram are versions of the same name and some scribes switched the spelling back and forth in an attempt to identify one king or the other.

> [22] Yet Edom revolted from under the hand of Judah unto this day. Then Libnah revolted at the same time.

The account of Israel and Judah separating and then coming apart little by little as time progressed plus the way corruption continued has a close parallel in the history of the church. First the split between east and west, then the Protestant Reformation, and now we have more than 30,000 denominations and sects, and even local independent churches continue to split and divide. One thing, however, that invariably tends to draw all true Christians together is persecution. We have more persecution of Christians today than at any other time in history with even more storm clouds brewing on the horizon.

²³ And the rest of the acts of Joram and all that he did, are they not written in the book of the chronicles of the kings of Judah?

²⁴ And Joram slept with his fathers and was buried with his fathers in the city of David, and Ahaziah, his son, reigned in his stead.

## From Bad to Worse in Judah

²⁵ In the twelfth year of Joram, the son of Ahab king of Israel, Ahaziah, the son of Jehoram king of Judah, began to reign.

²⁶ Ahaziah was twenty-two years old when he began to reign, and he reigned one year in Jerusalem. And his mother's name was Athaliah, the daughter of Omri, king of Israel.

²⁷ And he walked in the way of the house of Ahab and did evil in the sight of the LORD, as did the house of Ahab; for he was the son-in-law of the house of Ahab.

²⁸ And he went with Joram, the son of Ahab, to the war against Hazael, king of Syria, in Ramothgilead; and the Syrians wounded Joram.

²⁹ And king Joram went back to be healed in Jezreel of the wounds which the Syrians had given him at Ramah, when he fought against Hazael, king of Syria. And Ahaziah, the son of Jehoram king of Judah, went down to see Joram, the son of Ahab in Jezreel, because he was sick.

Joram (Jehoram) and Ahaziah never dreamed God might anoint their enemy to come against them. They thought they could continue to perform superficial rites and rituals, to use the name of God, and that nothing would ever happen to them.

Numerous people today believe they can do whatever they please and return to God whenever they please. This isn't the case. Those among the people of God who individually or corporately act knowingly against the will of God cannot return to God whenever they please. They can only return if God opens the door of repentance.

God was now setting the stage for a large confrontation. Two of the three elements he had promised to use were now in place. Elisha was fulfilling his function; Hazael, the enemy king, was anointed and had already inflicted a serious wound upon Jehoram, king of Israel. Now, God was about to place a new king over his people, Israel. This would happen abruptly and in a very different manner than anything that had ever happened before.

**Let us pray:**

Heavenly Father, we give you thanks for giving us clarity and understanding regarding the times we live in. We know that this story isn't just about Israel and Judah so many years ago, but that it is a message for us. That the real fulfillment is very close.

May we heed this important message and be found faithful at the time of the end. We ask this in the name of our Lord Jesus Christ. Amen.

# Chapter Fifteen
## Jezebel's Downfall

### 2 Kings 9

¹ Then Elisha, the prophet, called one of the sons of the prophets and said unto him, Gird up thy loins and take this flask of oil in thy hand and go to Ramothgilead.

² And when thou comest there, thou shalt see Jehu, the son of Jehoshaphat, the son of Nimshi, there; go in and make him arise up from among his brethren and take him to an inner chamber.

³ Then take the flask of oil and pour it on his head and say, Thus hath the LORD said, I have anointed thee king over Israel. Then open the door and flee and do not tarry.

Ramothgilead was a Levitical city of refuge located near where the Golan Heights, Israel, and Jordan come together today. Modern historians are unsure as to the exact location, but what they do know is that it was a strategic place for the defense of ancient Israel, and many battles were fought to claim it.

The young prophet was instructed to say, *Thus hath the LORD said,* because God had told Elijah to anoint Jehu more than twenty-five years before. This was a word the LORD had already given and would now be fulfilled.

Elisha, like Jesus, was prone to delegate important responsibility.

⁴ So the young man, the servant of the prophet, went to Ramothgilead.

⁵ And when he came, behold, the captains of the host were sitting, and he said, I have an errand to thee, O captain. And Jehu said, Unto which of all us? And he said, To thee, O captain.

The Hebrew word translated *Captain* can also be translated *Prince* or even *Priest*. The word denotes authority due to access to the presence of the king. This was a person who could come and go between the king and the people (or between the king and the army). This, in fact, is the origin of the word *Priest*. In Christ we are part of a royal priesthood. This is the priesthood of all believers.

> ⁶ And he arose and went into the house, and he poured the oil on his head and said unto him, Thus hath said the LORD God of Israel, I have anointed thee king over the people of Israel, even over Israel.

Ramothgilead means "a mound of testimony upon a high place." It was a marker or boundary of the inheritance of the people of God. It was here that Captain Jehu faithfully carried out his duty at his assigned post, when the full anointing suddenly came upon him. Jehu means "the LORD is he." Jehu also has a heavenly counterpart — Michael, meaning "who is like God" (If Daniel 12:1 and Matthew 13:41-43, 49-50 are parallel passages, major intervention from the heavenly hosts will take place at this time).

Up to this point we've seen what God had told Elijah and what Elisha told the young prophet to say. But the prophet continues to speak under the anointing, even after he poured the oil on the head of Jehu, for the Spirit of God was upon him.

> ⁷ And thou shalt smite the house of Ahab, thy master, that I may avenge the blood of my slaves, the prophets, and the blood of all the slaves of the LORD, at the hand of Jezebel.
>
> ⁸ For the whole house of Ahab shall perish, and I will cut off from Ahab him that pisses against the wall, he that is shut up as well as he that is left in Israel.
>
> ⁹ And I will make the house of Ahab like the house of Jeroboam, the son of Nebat, and like the house of Baasha, the son of Ahijah.
>
> ¹⁰ And the dogs shall eat Jezebel in the portion of Jezreel, and there shall be no one to bury her. And he opened the door and fled.

In the book of Revelation, we see a time when false religion is dealt a mortal blow. This occurs at the precise moment ordained by God (Revelation 11:15-19), but this moment also relates to a different prophetic ministry than what we've known until now in the church (Revelation 10, 11). This prophetic ministry with the Word of God won't come through anyone who still has problems with the old man.

This prophetic ministry will deliver a prophetic word through the new man in Christ — through a many-membered prophet who has a pure heart and the mind of Christ.

When the young prophet finished speaking, he took off running. He only said what God was saying and didn't add a single word of his own. Under these conditions and within the precise timing of God, this word went into immediate effect.

This is unlike most of the prophetic word we've had up to this point. They've been clean words followed by a long delay before being fulfilled. Most biblical prophecies are really focused on our time. In this passage, we see something very different. Consequences are much more immediate. They happen so fast that the messenger had to take off running. He gave the message in secret and fled. Within a few minutes, Ramothgilead would be locked down tight. No one would be allowed to go out.

> 11 Then Jehu came forth to the slaves of his lord, and one said unto him, Is there peace? Why did this mad fellow come to thee? And he said unto them, Ye know the man and his communication.
>
> 12 And they said, We know not; tell us now. And he said, Thus and thus he spoke unto me, saying Thus hath the LORD said, I have anointed thee king over Israel.

Jehu undoubtedly still had the anointing oil splattered all over him. I am told that the formula for a single portion of the anointing oil made two gallons (Exodus 30:23-25). If Elisha made a double portion (and this is likely the case), the prophet poured four gallons of oil over Jehu's head. Perhaps this was why the captains called the young prophet "this mad fellow."

When Jehu opened his mouth to speak this word, if it wasn't a true Word of the LORD, when King Joram found out about it, he would have immediately put Jehu to death along with any of his friends and relatives who looked suspicious.

> ¹³ Then they hastened, and each man took his garment, and put it under him in a high throne, and blew the shofar, saying, Jehu is king.

I believe this shofar or trumpet coincides with the seventh trumpet of Revelation 11:15. The consequences are similar.

What is the significance of their garments in this passage? This was a symbol of their authority and of the authority they are under — their covering. They took off their uniforms and made a throne for Jehu. This action showed they accepted that Jehu would reign over them. It also showed they were nullifying any previous commitment to King Joram.

> ¹⁴ So Jehu, the son of Jehoshaphat the son of Nimshi, conspired against Joram. Now Joram was keeping Ramothgilead, with all Israel, because of Hazael, king of Syria.

Note that Hazael helped set the stage for all of this.

> ¹⁵ But King Joram was returned to be healed in Jezreel of the wounds which the Syrians had given him, when he fought with Hazael, king of Syria. And Jehu said, If it is your desire, then do not let anyone go forth nor escape out of the city to tell the news in Jezreel.

> ¹⁶ So Jehu rode and went to Jezreel, for Joram lay there. And Ahaziah, king of Judah, was come down to see Joram.

Jezebel lived in Jezreel and ran most everything in Israel and Judah through Joram, her son, and Ahaziah, her son-in-law. Jezreel was about forty-two miles from Ramothgilead.

> ¹⁷ And the watchman, who stood in the tower of Jezreel, spied the company of Jehu as he came and said, I see a company. And Joram said, Take a horseman and send to meet them and let him say unto them, Is there peace?

¹⁸ So one on horseback went to meet him and said, Thus saith the king, Is there peace? And Jehu said, What hast thou to do with peace? Turn behind me. And the watchman gave notice, saying, The messenger came to them, but he does not return.

¹⁹ Then he sent out another on horseback, who came to them, and said, Thus saith the king, Is there peace? And Jehu answered, What hast thou to do with peace? Turn behind me.

²⁰ And the watchman gave notice again, saying, He also came unto them and does not return, and the pace of him who is coming is like the pace of Jehu, the son of Nimshi, for he comes impetuously.

²¹ And Joram said, Make ready. And his chariot was made ready. And Joram, king of Israel, and Ahaziah, king of Judah, went out, each in his chariot, and they went out to meet Jehu and found him in the portion of Naboth of Jezreel.

²² And when Joram saw Jehu, he said, Is there peace, Jehu? And he answered, What peace, so long as the fornications of thy mother Jezebel and her witchcrafts are so many?

The LORD has said he will bring about certain end-time judgments quickly. But today we have people prophesying and teaching that end-time tribulation and judgments will take a lot of time. Some say three and a half years and others say seven years.

In the examples of the book of Kings, we see a three-and-a-half-year famine prophesied by Elijah, followed by a seven-year famine prophesied by Elisha. However, when God decides to take out Jezebel and the corrupt kings of Israel and Judah, it only takes a few minutes. Within hours, the extended house of Ahab and all the worshippers of Baal are dead.

In Revelation, it says Babylon shall be thrown down with impetus and her plagues shall come in one day. All her riches shall come to nothing in one hour (Revelation 18:8-21).

It didn't take long for the prophet to arrive, pour the anointing oil over Jehu, and take off running. The other captains blew the shofar and made a throne with their garments, and Jehu left and rode to Jezreel, which wasn't too far away. It didn't take very long from the time Jehu was anointed to when both kings and Jezebel were dead.

Remember the story of righteous Naboth, the man murdered by Jezebel and Ahab so they could steal his vineyard? Jezreel means "God plants." Some who claim to operate in the name of the LORD have planted numerous evil things over the long history of Israel and the church. Now it's time for everyone to reap what they have sown. The harvest of what God has sown will also come to maturity, and then we'll see victory where at one time it appeared we were hopelessly defeated.

> 23 Then Joram turned his hands and fled and said to Ahaziah, There is treachery, O Ahaziah.

Those within the church who have done so much damage, persecuted so many sent in the name of the LORD, and haven't allowed the house of God to really be a house of prayer for all nations will turn and run when finally confronted by ministry commissioned by God for this purpose, but they won't be able to escape. Their "ecumenical" partners, like Ahaziah, won't be able to help them. Ecumenical means "in the family." Only two families matter: the family of Adam and the family of Christ; and they picked the wrong family.

> 24 But Jehu drew his bow with his full strength and smote Jehoram between his arms, and the arrow went out at his heart, and he sunk down in his chariot.
>
> 25 Then said Jehu to Bidkar, his captain, Take him and cast him in the edge of the portion of the field of Naboth of Jezreel. Remember that when thou and I went together after Ahab, his father, the LORD pronounced this sentence upon him, saying,
>
> 26 Surely I have seen yesterday the blood of Naboth and the blood of his sons, said the LORD, and I will requite thee in

this portion, said the LORD. Now, therefore, take and cast him into the portion, according to the word of the LORD.

Jehu knew the entire story.

²⁷ But when Ahaziah, the king of Judah, saw this, he fled by the way of the garden house. And Jehu followed after him and said, Smite him also in the chariot. And they did so at the ascent to Gur, which is by Ibleam. And he fled to Megiddo and died there.

This place had been Naboth's vineyard and Ahab turned it into a garden of herbs. Ahaziah attempted to flee *by the way of the garden house*. Adam and Eve were banished from the garden of God. Anyone attempting to return to the presence or place of God through carnal efforts (in the life we inherited from Adam) will be destroyed. Gur means "a lion's whelp" and Ibleam means "devouring people." Megiddo is the root of the famous term *Armageddon*, or literally *Har-Megiddo* (hill of the place of God).

Sundry prophecy teachers expect a last battle to be fought at Armageddon. Prior to this some think all Christians will be raptured to heaven. This is clearly not the case in this and every other prophetic example in Scripture. Megiddo is the site where those of the company of Jehu — of the true prince — finish off the enemies of God who have camouflaged themselves among the people of God. (Remember that key events take place in both the spiritual and the natural realms.) These enemies have even controlled the people of God like King Ahaziah.

This battle extends beyond the physical realm and into the spiritual. Elijah and Elisha (and whoever else had their eyes opened by God) continued to get glimpses of the heavenly hosts' chariots and horsemen of fire. In the natural world, of course, we also have signs that help us understand what's going on in the spiritual realm.

²⁸ And his slaves carried him to Jerusalem and buried him in his sepulchre with his fathers in the city of David.

²⁹ In the eleventh year of Joram, the son of Ahab, Ahaziah began to reign over Judah.

The king of Judah received a decent burial. Jezebel and the king of Israel did not.

## The Death of Jezebel

> ³⁰ And Jehu came to Jezreel, and when Jezebel heard of it, she painted her face and tired her head and looked out of a window.
>
> ³¹ And as Jehu entered in at the gate, she said, Had Zimri peace, who slew his master?

Jezebel's last words were another religious attempt to lay a guilt trip on someone. Jehu didn't argue with her though. It's rarely ever a good idea to argue with religious persons.

> ³² And he lifted up his face to the window and said, Who is on my side? Who? And two or three eunuchs looked at him.
>
> ³³ And he said, Throw her down. So they threw her down, and some of her blood was sprinkled on the wall and on the horses; and he trode her under foot.
>
> ³⁴ And he entered in, and after he ate and drank, he said, Go, see now this cursed woman and bury her; for after all she is a king's daughter.
>
> ³⁵ But when they went to bury her, they found no more of her than the skull and the feet and the palms of her hands.
>
> ³⁶ And they returned and told him. And he said, This is the word of the LORD, which he spoke by his slave Elijah, the Tishbite, saying, In the portion of Jezreel shall dogs eat the flesh of Jezebel.
>
> ³⁷ And the carcase of Jezebel shall be as dung upon the face of the field in the portion of Jezreel so that no one shall be able to say, This is Jezebel.

Compare this to the prophesied demise of Lucifer found in Isaiah 14:18-19.

> All the kings of the Gentiles, even all of them, lie in glory, each one in his own house. But thou art cast out of thy

grave like an abominable branch, and as the raiment of those that are slain, thrust through with a sword, that went down to the bottom of the pit, as a carcase trodden under feet.

Lest some think that this is just an out-of-date Old Testament story, in the New Testament Jesus says that Jezebel continues to be a problem in the church and this will also lead to drastic judgment.

> Notwithstanding I have a few things against thee because thou sufferest that woman Jezebel (who calls herself a prophetess) to teach and to seduce my slaves to commit fornication, and to eat things sacrificed to idols. (Revelation. 2:20)

This woman Jezebel also represents a group of people. They are sons of the devil who, as tares, are mixed with the people of God.

> And I have given her time to repent of her fornication, and she repented not. Behold, I will cast her into a bed and those that commit adultery with her into great tribulation unless they repent of their deeds. And I will kill her children with death. (Revelation 2:21-23)

It is Jezebel and her children who will be cast into great tribulation by the LORD. God doesn't destroy the righteous along with the wicked. This is when the true sons of God will shine (Daniel 12:3; Matthew 13:43).

We've been told many lies like how the great tribulation at the end of the age will get so bad God will have to secretly remove his people to heaven by rapture.

Yes, it is true God has removed his people from churches where lack of hearing the words of the LORD has created spiritual famine. But he has retained them and is sending them back because the time of famine is ending. When they return, history will become inverted, and those who have usurped the place of the Holy Spirit and wormed their way in among the people of God will suddenly be in mortal danger. This time God won't only destroy the prophets of Baal but also the worshippers of Baal from among his people.

This refers not only to those controlling the people of God; it also refers to those controlled by anyone other than God.

When God decides to do this, it will happen suddenly in one prophetic hour!

The devil isn't about to consolidate his kingdom and reign while the saints are whisked away to never-never land. The devil has already reigned over the world for six thousand years, and he can't do any better. He is unable to hold his divided kingdom together even when he operates as "queen" of Israel. At this time he will be defeated along with his sons and all of his worshippers. They will all be destroyed.

Brethren, the next prophetic events won't lead to a raptured church leaving a world without Christians where the devil consolidates a one world government, while some poor Jews who failed to repeat a sinner's prayer come into the great tribulation.

No! We've lived through centuries of martyrs, severe persecution, and much shed blood among the true prophets of God by Jezebel and her cohorts. God says they're going to answer for all the righteous blood they've shed, and when he turns the tables, it may take only one hour!

In the book of Daniel, we see this from another angle. When the great image that represents all the empires of man is destroyed, it happens suddenly when a stone cut without hands impacts the image. Then the stone, which is the kingdom of God, grows into a great mountain and covers the entire earth (Daniel 2:31-45).

The devil has introduced so many lies into the people of God that now he believes his own lies. If Jezebel and the two kings had known what was about to happen, they wouldn't have been sitting ducks. They never imagined what was about to happen until it was too late. God is about to do something with an anointing that hasn't been seen before. When he decides it is the right time, things will suddenly move forward.

> And at that time shall Michael stand up, the great prince who is for the sons of thy people, and it shall be a time of trouble, such as never was since there were people until

now, but in that time thy people shall escape, all those that were found written in the book.

And many of those that sleep in the dust of the earth shall be awakened, some for eternal life, and some for shame and everlasting confusion. And those that understand shall shine as the brightness of the firmament; and those that teach righteousness to the multitude as the stars in perpetual eternity. (Daniel 12:1-3)

And then in Malachi we read:

For, behold, the day comes that shall burn as an oven; and all the proud, and all that do wickedly shall be stubble; and the day that comes shall burn them up, said the LORD of the hosts, that it shall leave them neither root nor branch.

But unto you that fear my name shall the Sun of righteousness be born, and in his wings he shall bring saving health; and ye shall go forth and jump like calves of the herd.

And ye shall tread down the wicked; for they shall be ashes under the soles of your feet in the day that I make, said the LORD of the hosts. (Malachi 4:1-3)

And Matthew says:

As therefore the tares are gathered and burned in the fire, so shall it be at the end of this age. The Son of man shall send forth his angels, and they shall gather out of his kingdom all things that offend and those who do iniquity

and shall cast them into the furnace of fire; there shall be wailing and gnashing of teeth. Then shall the righteous shine forth as the sun in the kingdom of their Father. He who has ears to hear, let him hear. (Matthew 13:40-43)

**Let us pray:**

Heavenly Father, we thank you for your light and for your wisdom. We thank you for sharing your truth with those who are simple and humble.

May we take heed of your word for this hour and search our hearts that we might believe your word and be available to act when the time is right. We ask this in the name of the Lord Jesus Christ. Amen.

# Chapter Sixteen
## Baal Worship Is Eradicated out of Israel

### 2 Kings 10

¹ And Ahab had seventy sons in Samaria. And Jehu wrote letters and sent to Samaria unto the princes of Jezreel, to the elders, and to those that brought up Ahab's children, saying,

² Now as soon as this letter comes to you, unto those who have your master's sons and who have the chariots and horsemen and who have the arms and munitions of the city,

³ see which is the best and most upright of your master's sons and set him on his father's throne and fight for your master's house.

⁴ But they were exceedingly afraid and said, Behold, two kings could not stand before him; how then shall we stand?

Jehu killed two kings and Jezebel before he ate lunch. The next day, before many hours passed, all the sons of Ahab would be dead.

⁵ And he that was over the house and he that was over the city, the elders also, and those who had brought up the children sent to Jehu, saying, We are thy slaves and will do all that thou shalt bid us; we will not make any king; thou shalt do that which is good in thy eyes.

⁶ Then he wrote a letter the second time to them, saying, If ye are mine and if ye will hearken unto my voice, take the heads of the male sons of your master and come to me to Jezreel by tomorrow this time. Now the king's sons being seventy males, were with the great men of the city, who had brought them up.

After the murder of Naboth, God pronounced a sentence on the entire house of Ahab saying it would be completely wiped out. After Ahab humbled himself in sackcloth, God commuted the judgment and said it wouldn't take place during Ahab's lifetime but in his sons' time. Ahab's sons never repented. The closest they came was when Joram wore sackcloth under his royal robes during the siege of Samaria right before he attempted to kill the prophet Elisha.

> 7 And when the letter came to them, they took the king's sons and slew seventy males and put their heads in baskets and sent him them to Jezreel.
>
> 8 And a messenger came and told him, saying, They have brought the heads of the king's sons. And he said, Lay them in two heaps at the entrance of the gate until morning.
>
> 9 And in the morning, he went out and stood and said to all the people, Ye are righteous; behold, I conspired against my master and slew him; but who slew all these?
>
> 10 Know now that of the word of the LORD which the LORD spoke concerning the house of Ahab, nothing shall fall to the ground, for the LORD has done that which he spoke by his slave Elijah.
>
> 11 So Jehu slew all that had remained of the house of Ahab in Jezreel, and all his great men and all his kinsfolk and all his priests until he left him none remaining.

## The Pastor's Shearing House

> 12 And he arose and departed and came to Samaria. And as he was at a pastor's shearing house in the way,
>
> 13 Jehu met with the brethren of Ahaziah, king of Judah, and said, Who are ye? And they answered, We are the brethren of Ahaziah, and we go down to salute the sons of the king and the sons of the queen.
>
> 14 So he said, Take them alive. And after they took them alive, they slew them at the well of the shearing house, forty-two men, without leaving any.

The pastor's shearing house was the place where shepherds sheared or fleeced the sheep. Today we see many "pastors' shearing houses" where the sheep have been fleeced without mercy for quite some time. Judgment is about to fall. As explained earlier in this book, the number forty-two is symbolic of what must be corrected in man. Here we see exactly forty-two brethren of wicked King Ahaziah show up at the pastor's shearing house precisely as Jehu triumphantly made his way towards Samaria.

## Jehonadab, the Son of Rechab

> ¹⁵ And when he had departed from there, he met Jehonadab, the son of Rechab; and after he saluted him, he said to him, Is thy heart right as my heart is with thy heart? And Jehonadab answered, It is. If it is, give me thy hand. And he gave him his hand, and he took him up into the chariot.

The Rechabite clan always lived in tents and didn't drink wine. Jehonadab (mentioned also as Jonadab), the son of Rechab, brought up his sons in this manner. Generations later they still didn't deviate from their father's commandments. The LORD used them as an example many years later during the time of the prophet Jeremiah who asked, "If the Rechabites were able to follow the instructions of their father for so many generations, then why didn't the people of God follow the instructions of Father God?" (Jeremiah 35).

Jehonadab and King Jehu became friends, and Jehonadab accompanied the new king as he carried out the judgments of God against the house of Ahab and the worshippers of Baal.

> ¹⁶ And he said, Come with me, and thou shalt see my zeal for the LORD. So they had him ride in his chariot.
>
> ¹⁷ And when he came to Samaria, he slew all that had remained of Ahab in Samaria, until he had completely destroyed him, according to the word of the LORD which he had spoken to Elijah.

When God sends forth judgment and people are put to death, it is always done on the basis of at least two or three witnesses (Deuteronomy 17:6; Matthew 18:16). Jehonadab was another trustworthy witness at the side of Jehu as the judgments upon the house of Ahab and the worshippers of Baal fell.

## The Worshippers of Baal

<sup>18</sup> And Jehu gathered all the people together and said unto them, Ahab served Baal a little but Jehu shall serve him much.

<sup>19</sup> Now, therefore, call unto me all the prophets of Baal, all his servants, and all his priests; let no one be lacking, for I have a great sacrifice to do to Baal; whoever is lacking shall not live. But Jehu did it in subtilty to the intent that he might destroy those that served Baal.

<sup>20</sup> And Jehu said, Sanctify a solemn assembly for Baal. And they proclaimed it.

<sup>21</sup> And Jehu sent though all Israel and all the worshippers of Baal came, so that there was no one lacking that did not come. And they came into the house of Baal, and the house of Baal was full from one end to another.

<sup>22</sup> And he said to the one that was over the vestry. Bring forth vestments for all those that serve Baal. And he brought them forth vestments.

In Baal worship (the god of worldly prosperity), the vestments or covering were a big deal. Jehu had all the worshippers of Baal put on their vestments. This further helped identify all the worshippers of Baal so no one would be killed by mistake.

Starting with King Joram, King Ahaziah, Jezebel, and following with the sons of Ahab and the brothers of Ahaziah and then all the worshippers of Baal — none of them had any advance warning that they were about to be killed. This is how it will be at the end of this age.

<sup>23</sup> And Jehu went with Jehonadab the son of Rechab, into the house of Baal and said unto the servants of Baal,

> Search and make sure that none of the slaves of the LORD are here with you, but only the servants of Baal.

Jehu even had the servants of Baal search to make sure none of the servants of the LORD were present. He wanted to be sure no innocent person was killed. Jesus will be even more careful when he returns.

> ²⁴ And when they went in to offer sacrifices and burnt offerings, Jehu put eighty men outside and said, Whoever leaves alive any of the men whom I have brought into your hands, his life shall be for that of the other.

Eighty men — eight is the number of new beginnings and ten has to do with the law. Contrary to popular belief in much of the church, God is about to apply the law in judgment to all the tares (sons of the evil one) that have been planted by the enemy in and among the wheat; he will bring about a new beginning by removing the wicked from among the righteous. True sons and daughters of God who are led by the Spirit of God aren't under the law (Romans 8:14; Galatians 5:18), and it is only those who are led by the Spirit of God that God will keep completely safe in the coming time of upheaval.

Jehu made sure all the people he and his men would kill put on the vestments of Baal and took part in offering sacrifices and burnt offerings to Baal. In the near future, when God brings judgment against those in Israel and the church who are worshipping the god of prosperity of this world, instead of or along with the LORD, he will also make sure there are at least two or three witnesses against each person destroyed in the judgment.

> ²⁵ And after they had finished offering the burnt offering, Jehu said to those of his guard and to the captains, Go in, and slay them; let none escape. And they smote them with the edge of the sword, and the guard and the captains left them where they fell and went to the city of the house of Baal.

Many houses of worship today look like churches, but in reality they are houses of Baal. None of them will survive the coming judgment.

²⁶ And they removed the images out of the house of Baal and burned them.

²⁷ And they broke down the image of Baal and broke down the house of Baal and made it a latrine unto this day.

²⁸ Thus Jehu destroyed Baal out of Israel.

The judgments God prophesied to Elijah regarding Israel, the house of Ahab, and the worshippers of Baal didn't happen over a long, drawn-out period of time. From the time the young prophet anointed Jehu to the total destruction of Ahab's house with its tentacles and the destruction of all of the worshippers of Baal (not a single one of them was left alive in Israel), about seventy-two hours could have transpired.

If you read the rest of 2 Kings 10, you see that Jehu wasn't perfect. In fact, he had some serious flaws just like Gideon and many others used by God in the Old Testament. Yet if we have discernment, we can read between the lines of this story and receive insight into end-time events that will take place soon.

Jehonadab means "the LORD is generous." When the Lord Jesus returns, what if we were to meet him like Jehonadab met Jehu? When we meet him in the air, will Jesus pull up in the fiery chariot surrounded with the fiery horsemen Elijah and Elisha saw? Will he extend his hand and take us with him as he executes righteous judgment upon the earth? What will happen when we pull up with Jesus at a nearby pastor's shearing house and confront the brothers of "Ahaziah"? What will happen when we pull into the local house of Baal right in the midst of the Sunday morning worship service?

**Let us pray:**

Heavenly Father, we ask that these things might be clear to us in the measure that our hearts are clean before you. We ask this in the name of our Lord Jesus Christ. Amen.

# Meet the Author

At the age of four, while his family was living in Minneapolis, Minnesota, Russell Stendal prayed and asked God to call his parents, Chad and Pat, to be missionaries. God answered that prayer and within just a few years the whole family was on the mission field in Colombia, South America. He became an accomplished jungle pilot and married a beautiful Colombian lady named Marina. They have four children, Lisa, Alethia, Russell Jr., and Dylan, plus six grandchildren.

When Russell was 27 years old, Marxist guerrillas of the FARC kidnapped him for 142 days. The story of his kidnapping is told in the book he wrote titled *Rescue the Captors*. His reason for the title is because he realized that his captors were more captive than he was. There was a possibility he would be released, but most of his kidnappers were young people who had been taken from their families, given a weapon, and taught to kill. They had little hope of survival.

To reach all the actors of the armed conflict, including his former captors, Russell established a radio ministry to air programs into the dangerous war stricken areas of Colombia with messages of peace and hope. He has also written more than 50 books in English and Spanish.

In 2017, he was awarded the Shahbaz Bhatti Freedom Award, (given to Pope Francis the year before) for his tireless efforts towards spreading peace and reconciliation in Colombia (in the context of promoting religious freedom). Russell travels extensively as a guest speaker in conventions around the world. His speaking is unique in that he is very sensitive to the Lord's voice and does not hesitate to deliver the message imparted to him, no matter how uncomfortable that may be to him or to others. Most of the books he has published were transcribed directly from the radio messages he has preached in Spanish and beamed into virtually all of the war torn areas of the countryside.

Russell is the editor of the Jubilee Bible translation that has been published in English and in Spanish. Well over a million copies of this Bible have been donated and distributed into the most needy areas of Colombia and Venezuela.

Please leave a review of this book on Amazon. Whether one star or five, your input is important to us.

For Questions or Comments, please contact us at:
https://ransompressinternational.com/contact-us/

# More Titles by this Author

**Rescue the Captors**
The true story of a kidnapped jungle pilot, written from within a Marxist guerrilla camp in rural Colombia, South America

**Rescue The Captors 2**
Faith That Can Move Mountains

**The Hidden Agenda (Rescue the Captors 3)**
An Extraordinary True Story Behind Colombia's Peace Negotiations with the FARC

**God's Plan for Spiritual Battle**
Victory Over Sin, the World, and the Devil

**The Book of Daniel**
and other related prophecies

**The Morning Star**
A Message to the Church

**The Seventh Trumpet & The Seven Thunders**
God's Prophetic Plan Revealed

**What About the Church?**
What God desires from his people in the end times

**The Correction Factor: Zechariah**
A Key to Unlock The Book of Revelation

**The River of God**
Blessings from the Throne to the Uttermost Parts of the Earth

**The Mystery of the Will of God**
A Message to the Persecuted Church

**Queen Esther & The Ring of Power**
Prophetic Voice for the End Times

**Revelation Unveiled**
Understanding the Heart of Jesus In the Imminent Day of the Lord

**Uncovering What Religion Has to Hide**
The Testimony of Simon Peter

**Elijah & Elisha**
The Mantle for God's People

**The Philosophy of King Solomon**
Hidden Wisdom from Ecclesiastes

**Preparing for The End of the World**
    Writings from the Apostle Paul to the Thessalonians
    Regarding the End Times

**Wisdom for the End Times**
    A Commentary from the Book of Proverbs

**Faith and Grace**
    Reflections on the Letter of Saint Paul to the Romans

**The Gospel of Jesus Christ: Whosoever Will Come After Me ...**
    A Study in Mark

**Counted Faithful**
    Rebuilding the "Wall" and the "Gates" of the City of God

**Joshua and the Promised Land**
    Entering the Fullness of our Inheritance in Christ

**The Unquenchable Life**
    What the Apostles Teach Us About Victorious Christian Living

**Knowing God the Father**
    A Commentary on the Gospel and Epistles of John

**Job and the Place of Understanding**
    A Study in Ancient Philosophy

**Ruth**
    A Prophetic Story of Faith, Grace, and Redemption

**The Time of Correction**
    And the Promise of the Eternal Inheritance

**Discerning the Day of the Lord**
    Convergence of End Time Prophecies in the Book of Isaiah

**The Promise of Our Father**
    Of Purity, Power, and Unity in the Holy Spirit

**Toward an Exceeding and Eternal Weight of Glory**
    A Study of the Pauline Epistles to the Corinthians and Timothy

**The Prize of the High Calling of God**
    A concise study of Galatians, Ephesians,
    Philippians, Colossians, Titus, and Philemon

**The Generation of Christ**
    A Study of the Gospel of Matthew

Many of Russell's books are also available in Spanish. See Amazon for all his titles, including eBooks and Audiobooks.

# Stendal Family Ministries

Ransom Press International and Colombia Para Cristo Society are owned and operated by the Stendal family. It is at the heart of our ministry to share the powerful message of the Word of God with as many people as possible, and to make the Holy Scriptures freely available to every person on the face of the planet, beginning with those who have the least access to a Bible.

Please look through the following pages to see what we are doing, how we are doing it, and to discover if there is a way in which you might want to help us serve our Lord Jesus Christ.

# Ransom Press International Publishing Mission

In March of 2020, the Stendals reopened their publishing house so they could best manage costs and logistics, and with the Lord's seemingly infinite provision of persons and organizations, make their publications more freely available than ever before. To learn more about Ransom Press International, please visit our website at: https://ransompressinternational.com

## Jubilee Bible Distribution

The *Jubilee Bible* and *Biblia del Jubileo* can be obtained free of charge in eBook format across various eReader platforms and websites. Print editions of the *Jubilee Bible* and *Biblia del Jubileo* are distributed a bit differently. The *Jubilee Bible* is available in limited retail quantity, whereas the *Biblia del Jubileo* is largely distributed free of cost to the impoverished. When sold at retail, all net proceeds are spent on expenses for free distribution, such as our Bibles for Venezuela Project in partnership with SOM International™. Audiobook format is also available through Amazon Audible®.

## Christian Book and Media Distribution

Ransom Press International's Christian book and media distribution are handled much the same as our Bible distribution. For those who prefer Kindle and other select eReader platforms, the cost is $0.99 to $2.99 for eBooks. Print-on-demand and audiobooks typically cost more. As with our Bibles, all net proceeds are placed back into ministry to help cover the cost of free distribution to remote and impoverished areas of the world.

## Questions or Comments?

If you have any difficulty locating our Bibles or publications for an affordable amount, please contact us at:

https://ransompressinternational.com/contact-us/

## Colombia Para Cristo Society

https://cpcsociety.ca

### Stendal Latin America Ministry

For information on the Stendal's Latin America Ministry and to find out the latest news, how to get involved, and how to pray for Colombia and Venezuela, please visit our CPC Society website.

**Prayer Alerts**
https://cpcsociety.ca/prayer-alerts/

**Be a Part**
https://cpcsociety.ca/be-a-part/

CPC Society

## Spirit of Martyrdom International

https://spiritofmartyrdom.com

## Supporting Persecuted Christians

SOM International™ raises awareness and support for believers all over the world who are at risk because of their faith in Jesus Christ. Founded by David Witt in 2004, SOM International™ places 100% of designated funds into the hands of leaders serving in the riskiest and most unreached areas in the world.

Additionally, SOM International™ plays an integral role in the Stendal Family's ministries by managing their charitable income, producing quality media-content, and partnering in the distribution of Bibles and Christian literature through the SOM Bookstore and the Bibles for Venezuela Project.

Through the SOM Bookstore, you may obtain Ransom Press International publications (print or eBook) for a free will offering of any amount, and 100% of all proceeds will go to directly to support the Bibles for Venezuela Project at: https://spiritofmartyrdom.com/biblesforvenezuela/.

SOM International
Bibles for Venezuela

SOM International
Newsletter

## Receive Newsletter Updates

Stay apprised of the Bibles for Venezuela Project. Sign up for our newsletter at: https://spiritofmartyrdom.com/application-form/

## Get Involved

Learn about the many ways that Spirit of Martyrdom International™ is supporting not only the Stendal's Latin America Ministry, but also numerous ministries that serve the Church at risk, across the globe. Join us at: https://spiritofmartyrdom.com/get-involved/

# Jubilee Bible (JUB)

The Jubile Bible Website

SOM International Bookstore

Download for Free at:
www.sombookstore.com/
or
www.thejubileebible.org/get/

## The Jubilee Bible
### From the Scriptures of the Reformation

Translated from the Original Texts in Hebrew and Greek into Spanish by Casiodoro de Reina (1569) and compared with the revision of Cipriano de Valera (1602).

Based on the New Testament of Francisco de Enzinas (1543) and on the New Testament (1556) with the Psalms (1557) of Juan Pérez de Pineda.

This material was translated from Spanish into English by Russell M. Stendal and compared with the Old English Translation of William Tyndale (Pentateuch of 1530, Ploughboy Edition New Testament of 1534, Joshua to 2 Chronicles of 1537, and Jonah). Also compared word for word with the Authorized Version (by King James) of 1611.

*The word of our God shall stand for ever.* (Isaiah 40:8)

### Why this Version?

The Jubilee Bible (JUB) stands apart from most other English versions in print since the beginning of the last century. The usage and context tend to define each key word so you do not have to blindly rely on theological dictionaries or reference materials that may wittingly or unwittingly include any type of prejudice or bias.

Careful attention in properly and consistently translating each key word, through the first usage and on through to the last occurrence, was made to avoid the use of synonyms. Then, as the word makes its way across the Old Testament and you make the correct match with the corresponding Greek word in the New Testament, an amazing pattern emerges.

The Jubilee Bible is the only translation we know of that has made a serious attempt to mate each unique Hebrew word (and subsequently its Greek equivalent) with a unique English word (using the common English of William Tyndale and the extraordinary Hebrew scholarship of Casiodoro de Reina of the early Reformation) so that the use (and number of occurrences of each key word) sets forth the idea of what God means by each word as defined by the actual context in Scripture.

## The Importance of Linguistics

Have you ever come across footnotes in the Old Testament that say, "Hebrew obscure" or "Hebrew uncertain"? This is not due to any lack of content or clarity in the original text, but rather to the fact that most modern Hebrew scholars simply do not know the precise meaning of many of the original idioms with any degree of certainty. For hundreds of years, Hebrew was studied as a "dead" language (a language that was not spoken in everyday life). The difference between studying a "living" versus a "dead" language could be compared to the difference between studying fossils or museum exhibits of long-extinct animals versus studying living examples of the same species.

A number of years ago, I was given a copy of an old Spanish Bible translated in the heat and fervor of the Reformation (which was brutally put down in Spain by the Inquisition) during a time when it was common practice to burn Bibles along with their owners. I immediately began to notice a depth and clarity to this translation that brought forth a clear witness of the Spirit of God as to the meanings of many seemingly unfathomable passages (mainly in the Psalms, Proverbs, and Prophets) that had intrigued me for years. I began to investigate the unique circumstances of this Spanish translation by Casiodoro de Reina, published in 1569.

Casiodoro de Reina was born in 1520. He learned Hebrew in Spain as a young man, apparently from Jews who still spoke Hebrew as a "living" language. The Jews had been officially expelled from Spain in 1492, but it is estimated that only one-fourth of them left at that time (some of those who remained did their best to blend in with the Christians). Eventually the Spanish Inquisition made it impossible for any Jewish people, who spoke their own language, to survive in Spain. Almost every Hebrew scholar since Casiodoro de Reina has had to learn Hebrew as a "dead" language, which was no longer spoken, until the modern-day, ongoing resurrection of the Hebrew language in Israel.

Casiodoro began a translation of the Old Testament from Hebrew to Spanish and was forced to flee from Spain in 1551. Several Jewish translations of the Old Testament were published in Spanish about this time (such as the *Biblia de Ferrara* of 1553) to which Casiodoro had access. He also built on a translation of Psalms that was published by his friend Juan Pérez de Pineda in 1557. He went to Geneva and was there until the government of Geneva under John Calvin burned Miguel Servet at the stake over differences on points of doctrine. Casiodoro had some strong words about this. He said that Geneva had become a "new Rome," and he left for England. The Queen of England (Elizabeth I) allowed Casiodoro to preach to Spanish speakers in the Church of St. Mary Axe and gave him a monthly income. Casiodoro continued his Bible translation until the Inquisition found out about it and sent agents from Spain, who brought false charges against him and undermined his support from the Queen.

Casiodoro fled to Germany just in time to witness a war between Lutherans and Catholics. He had some words with the Lutherans regarding this and went on into the Low Countries. There he was given a place to preach in a Congregational Church where he spent quite a bit of time in conflict with the Consistory (the minutes of those meetings still exist). Casiodoro seemed to always maintain an open mind to truth and refused to go along with any given school of doctrine or thought, believing that everyone must be responsible before God for their own conscience. After more than twenty years of working on his translation while fleeing with his wife and children—always staying just one jump ahead of the Inquisition, which was always sending agents to attempt to kill or hinder him—his Bible was finally printed. The Inquisition set up a ring of *retenes,* or checkpoints, all along the borders and for many years carefully searched every person and/or cargo that entered

Spain, making an all-out effort to not let even one single Bible into the country. They searched for Bibles with the same intensity that our modern countries search passengers for weapons and drugs! Casiodoro was last heard of at age seventy, still one jump ahead of the Inquisition, and it is not known for certain whether they got him in the end or not.

Casiodoro de Reina, although younger, was a contemporary with William Tyndale. I have noticed many similarities between the translations of both men (William Tyndale in English and Casiodoro de Reina in Spanish). Studying these two Bibles (they basically agree, yet each brings out unique facets of truth from a slightly different perspective) has been the equivalent of getting the truth of the Scriptures of the Reformation in stereo. The power and clarity of their translations has a much sharper edge than the work that was done in either language even a generation later when the intense heat of the Reformation had died down, and Bible translation had to be officially approved by ecclesiastic and/or secular governments.

It is recognized that the Authorized Version (by King James) in English is basically a revision of Tyndale's work (in many key passages the wording of the AV is ninety percent or more Tyndale's), with the exception of the last half of the Old Testament (from Ezra to Malachi). This portion of Tyndale's work is believed to have been lost at sea in a shipwreck (only the book of Jonah survived). Unfortunately, William Tyndale was burned at the stake before he could redo the books that were lost. This disaster has, in my opinion, placed these books of our English AV Bibles on a foundation less than equal in terms of clarity and consistency of translation with the rest of the AV, which draws so extensively from the work of Tyndale.

When we edited a recent edition of the Spanish Bible (*Las Sagradas Escrituras Version Antigua*, or *Biblia del Jubileo*) based on the original text of Casiodoro de Reina, I checked much of it against the work of William Tyndale and against the Authorized Version. This strengthened the Spanish Bible in many areas and also tended to confirm the opinion that I gave in the preceding paragraph. Then I decided to diligently compare and align the work of Casiodoro de Reina with the books of the Authorized Version, which did not receive the heritage of William Tyndale.

The first fruit of that endeavor is this rendition of Psalms, Proverbs, Ecclesiastes, and Song of Solomon.

Over the years, there have been many revisions of the Authorized Version. Some of these, under the guise of modernizing the language, have watered down the message and introduced errors proceeding from deviant manuscripts, from doctrines of men, and from over simplification of the English language. The same is true regarding the Spanish Bible. Instead of revising "forward" toward modernism and employing modern scholarship, textual criticism, and the like, it has been our intention to revise "back" and return as close as possible to the roots of the pure message and pure language. I believe we are at a place where brilliant scholarship and linguistics alone cannot discern between all the possible variations of meaning, or among what are all being presented as ancient and worthy manuscripts in the original languages. We must have the witness of the Holy Spirit. I have chosen to go with the Hebrew scholarship of Reformers such as William Tyndale and Casiodoro de Reina, whose translations of the Received Text (*Textus Receptus*) shined the light of the truth into the spiritual darkness of their day and changed the church and the world for the better, rather than to rely on the modern scholarship that has a penchant for removing the fear of the Lord from among the people of God in this Laodicean hour.

Let us allow the Spirit of Truth to have the last word regarding this matter. We must always bear in mind that even if we were to all learn Hebrew to perfection and could obtain a flawless manuscript of the original text, there would still be a humanly insurmountable language barrier between us and the truth that can only be bridged by the Spirit of God.

— **Russell M. Stendal** (Translator and Editor)

*For with thee is the fountain of life: in thy light shall we see light.*
(Psalm 36:9)

# Editor's Notes

Of the original edition of Casiodoro de Reina, we only know of a handful of copies that survived the fire of the Spanish Inquisition. Many Bibles were burned together with their owners. William Tyndale was killed because he translated, published, and distributed the Word of God. But when the devil knew that he could not stop subsequent editions of the Holy Scriptures, he was obligated to change his tactics. Taking advantage of the good intentions of many to actualize, modernize, and simplify the Bible, the Enemy was able to plant his tares, partially dim the light and truth of the Word of God, and little by little, dull the sword of the Christian.

It is our intention to actualize orthography and grammar only to the extent that we are confident that the original full range of meaning can be preserved; that we may deliver to you a translation that contains all the force and anointing that was poured out in the sixteenth century over men like Francisco de Encinas, Juan Pérez de Pineda, Casiodoro de Reina, Cipriano de Valera, and William Tyndale — men who were chosen by God to be translators of the Bible.

Keeping to the tradition of these reformers, we have continued to take great care to ensure that key terminology is translated in a uniform manner and to footnote exceptions. These features also make this an outstanding Bible to study by computer. The first usage, last usage, and development of each key term has been carefully checked (the number of overall instances and number of verses in which a given term is used have been carefully tabulated and tracked to ensure separation of terminology and to eliminate the use of synonyms wherever possible within the limits of the English language). This means that when you print a list of all the occurrences of a given term or phrase and study these verse lists, this Bible then defines itself, and the exact value that God has placed on each key term can be established beyond the shadow of a doubt without the need to look up the meanings of the words in a dictionary or commentary that may have been tainted by human endeavor (which in some cases could also be slanted according to the doctrine or school of thought of those who compiled the material).

We have also made an effort to preserve the emphasis of the original translators in our use of capitals and words in italics. Italics are used when the translator considered the word to be necessary in order to complete a proper translation of the thought or phrase, but the word does not appear in the manuscript of the original language. Words enclosed in curly brackets are explanations amplified by the translator to avoid misunderstandings. The punctuation and orthography have the principal purpose of preserving the meaning, flow, and unity of the original manuscripts and do not always follow the norm of modern English.

The **Name of God** appears in the Hebrew manuscripts of the Holy Scriptures with four consonants (without vowels) **YHWH** or **JHVH** and translates literally into English as **I AM** (according to Exodus 3:14). This is expressed in like manner in Greek in various New Testament texts (see Matthew 14:27; Mark 14:62; Luke 22:70; John 4:26; 6:35, 41; 8:18, 24, 28, 58; 11:25; 18:5-8; Revelation 1:8, 11, 17; 2:23; 21:6; 22:13, 16). The ancients considered that the **Name of God** was too sacred to pronounce, and so they read *Adonai* or *Lord* each time that they encountered the four consonants of the tetragrammaton. This tradition was followed by our Lord Jesus and by the apostles in more than three hundred instances when they were quoting the Scriptures of the Old Testament. In this work, for the most part, we have continued in the tradition of our Lord Jesus in regard to the **Name of God** (**YHWH**) in the Old Testament. If the original read **YHWH**, the translation reads **LORD**. If the original read **Adonai**, the translation reads **Lord**. If the original read **Adonai YHWH**, the translation reads **Lord GOD**. In a few instances (such as Exodus 3:14), the tetragrammaton is translated **I AM**.

## Translator's Notes

**Amen** — "So be it".

**Belial** — Satan; the Evil One.

**Charity** — The original translators used this term to differentiate God's love {Gr. ágape} from man's love {Gr. phileos}. God's love is born of sacrifice (not of human emotion), and is redemptive by nature. God the Father gave us his only Son, Jesus — in turn, Jesus gave his life for us. Only God can put this type of redemptive love within us; we are not capable of this on our own (see 1 Corinthians Chapter 13).

**Chasten** — The primary meaning is to refine or to purify, and comes from the root word, chaste.

**Congregation** — In the Old Testament, "congregation" is not italicized, and is inclusive of all of God's people, Israel. In the New Testament, "congregation" is italicized to translate the Greek word, "ekklesia", which literally means called out ones. This applies to, and includes, individuals, small or large groups, and even the universal body of Christ.

**Earth and Land** — Both are the same word in the original language. Spiritually, this has to do with the entire People of God (Israel and the Church).

**Eternal** — The primary meaning denotes a change in quality (like a change of state). The secondary meaning denotes unlimited time as the result of coming into another realm (God's realm). Therefore, eternal life is not life in the human quality that we inherited from Adam, going on forever; rather, it is a new quality of life in Jesus Christ, which may begin now for those who are born again by the Spirit of God.

**Fools** — Those who are governed by carnal thoughts and desires. This is folly in God's eyes.

**Halelu** — "Praise ye".

**Jubilee** — The primary meaning is freedom; liberty. The secondary meaning is the joy of being set free.

**Life and Soul** — Both are the same word in the original language. They are translated either one way or the other, according to context.

**Right Hand** — Authority (power; strength).

**Selah** — "Stop and think about it". "Meditate on this".

**Shadow** — Spiritually, this has the connotation of covering and protection.

**Sheol {Heb.} Hades {Gr.}** — This is the empire of the first death, under the power of Satan, which imprisoned even the justified souls until the redemptive work of Jesus, and continues to retain every unjustified soul as they await final judgment. This is different from the lake of fire or Gehena (Hell), of the final judgment, which is the second death (See Luke 16:20–31; Ephesians 4:8; Revelation 20:14).

**Shofar** — A special ram's horn trumpet, blown on the Day of Atonement to announce the year of Jubilee, and on other particular occasions, including battle and for warning.

**Spirit and Wind and Breath** — All three are the same word in the original language. Translated according to context.

**Unicorn** — Meaning, one horn. In the old Spanish this is the Rhinoceros.

**Usage of Italics** — In the Scripture text, italicized words were added by the translator for either proper English or for clarification.

**Usage of Certain Pronouns** —

**Thee, Thou, Thy:** always singular in meaning.

> **Note:** serious doctrinal error can result from the consequences of changing Thee, Thou, or Thy to You or Your (you and your can be ambiguous regarding singularity). This can cause scriptural promises or directives addressed to the individual to be mistakenly applied to a corporate group. Modern English is ambiguous in this regard and lacks the precision necessary to accurately render the true meaning of the original.

**Ye:** always plural in meaning and denoting a corporate or plural situation.

> **Note:** serious doctrinal error can result from the consequences of changing ye to you and then indiscriminately applying scriptural promises or directives that apply corporately to the People of God to a given individual. Modern English has lost this important distinction.

The Jubilee Bible
(from the Scriptures of the Reformation)
Copyright © 2024
by Russell M. Stendal

All rights reserved.

May be quoted in other works. May be used freely in all non-profit, non-commercial Bible distribution endeavors provided the content is not altered. For all commercial reproduction, express written permission from the publisher is required.

Ransom Press International and logos are trademarks of,
Ransom Press International
4918 Roosevelt Street
Hollywood, Florida, 33021

ISBN: 978-1-64765-022-3
eBook ISBN: 978-1-64765-087-2

For questions or comments please visit:
www.ransompressinternational.com/contact-us/

# The Jubilee Bible
# Dictionary & Concordance

The Jubile Bible Website

SOM International Bookstore

Download for Free at:
www.sombookstore.com/
or
www.thejubileebible.org/get/

*The Jubilee Bible: Dictionary & Concordance* is a companion resource that enhances the study of the Holy Scriptures by guiding the reader in discovering the meaning and significance of proper Greek and Hebrew names, as well as important words used throughout the Bible. While the reader will find this dictionary and concordance applicable to nearly any English version of the Bible, the concordance is especially effective when studying the *Jubilee Bible* (JUB). This is because the translation of the *Jubilee Bible* stands apart from most other versions printed since the beginning of the last century.

In the *Jubilee Bible* (JUB) the usage and context tend to define each key word so you don't have to blindly rely on theological dictionaries or reference materials that may, wittingly or unwittingly, include any type of prejudice or bias. Careful attention in properly and consistently translating each key word, through the first usage and on through to the last occurrence, was made to avoid the use of synonyms. Then, as the word makes its way across the Old Testament and you make the correct match with the corresponding Greek word in the New Testament, an amazing pattern emerges.

The *Jubilee Bible* is the only translation we know of that has made a serious attempt to mate each unique Hebrew word (and subsequently its Greek equivalent) with a unique English word (using the common English of William Tyndale and the extraordinary Hebrew scholarship of Casiodoro de Reina of the early Reformation), so that the usage (and number of occurrences of each key word) sets forth the idea of what God means by each word, as defined by the actual context in Scripture.

# Biblia del Jubileo (JBS)
## (Spanish Edition)

The Jubile Bible Website

SOM International Bookstore

Download for Free at:
www.sombookstore.com/
or
www.thejubileebible.org/get/

## La Biblia del Jubileo
### Originales en Hebreo y Griego

Traducida de los Textos Originales en hebreo y griego al español por Casiodoro de Reina (1569) y comparada con la revisión de Cipriano de Valera (1602).

Basada en el Nuevo Testamento de Francisco de Enzinas (1543) y en el Nuevo Testamento (1556) con los Salmos (1557) de Juan Pérez de Pineda; por último, cotejado con la primera traducción al inglés de William Tyndale (Nuevo Testamento de 1534) y con la Versión Autorizada (King James) de 1611.

*La Palabra del Dios nuestro permanece para siempre. (Isaías 40:8)*

La Biblia del Jubileo
Editado por: Russell M. Stendal
Biblia del Jubileo 2000 © 2000, 2001, 2010, 2014, 2017, 2020, 2023

Puede citarse en otras obras. Siempre que su contenido no sea alterado, puede utilizarse libremente en la distribución sin fines de lucro y no comercial de la Biblia. Se necesita permiso escrito de los editores para su reproducción comercial.

Editorial Ransom Press International y Logos son marcas registradas de Ransom Press International, Inc.

Ransom Press International
4918 Roosevelt Street
Hollywood, Florida, 33021

ISBN: ISBN: 978-1-64765-089-6
libro electronico ISBN: 978-1-64765-017-9

visite: www.ransompressinternational.com y www.martinstendal.com

# Study the Jubilee Bibles Online at Bible Gateway & YouVersion

**Bible Gateway Apps**

**Bible Gateway**

Bible Gateway has an especially good interface for study and in-depth searching of the of the Jubilee Bible (JUB) and Biblia del Jubileo (JBS), and offers free online access and the Bible Gateway Mobile Apps: https://biblegateway.com/app/

**YouVersion Apps**

Read the *Jubilee Bible* (JUB) and *Biblia del Jubileo* (JBS) for free on YouVersion, or download and read them for free using their YouVersion Bible Apps: https://youversion.com/the-bible-app/.

# Listen to Radio Colombia para Cristo
## (formerly, Fuereza de Paz Radio)

Over 20 years ago, an American pilot was kidnapped by Colombian guerrillas. During his captivity in the Colombian jungle, the idea to *Rescue his Captors* emerged. Fuerzadepaz is the answer to those who allow God to be the one to judge. With this application, you'll have access to hundreds of recorded messages, tens of books, and a radio signal.

## Get the Radio Colombia Para Cristo Apps for Browser & Android

https://tustreaming.co/AUDIO/CPC/

https://play.google.com/store/apps/details?id=com.creativoagencia.rcpc&hl=en_CA&gl=US

## Listen to Jubilee Radio

Jubilee Radio is a compilation of music and Scripture portions in audio read directly from the Jubilee Bible. The music is also an attempt to go back and rescue those good, old, soulful songs now almost forgotten, instead of giving into the noise of modern evangelical music.

### Get the Jubilee Radio App
### for iPhone & Android

https://tustreaming.co/AUDIO/JUBILEE/

https://play.google.com/store/apps/details?id=com.jubilee.radio

## Audio-Video Ministry

Russell Stendal teaches through the books of the Bible via broadcasts on radio and YouTube. During the lockdown of the COVID-19 pandemic he completed a series of messages on the Book of Isaiah, which are now available in their entirety on YouTube. Be sure to look for future multimedia productions from Ransom Press International

### Russell Stendal YouTube Channel

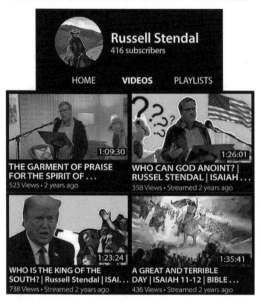

Watch Russell Stendal's teaching series on the Book of Isaiah and more, at:

https://youtube.com/channel/UCrE7aGspNt_aVqFQkHLJAIw/videos

## La Montaña — Feature Film

A Colombian movie written and directed by
Alethia and Lisa Stendal

(Subtitled in English)

### YouTube
https://youtu.be/elKostRbNOw

### SOM International™ on DVD
https://sombookstore.com/product/la-montana/

### Amazon on DVD
https://amazon.com/dp/B00CT4YQ3W

On a mountain in Colombia, paramilitary forces have Marxist rebels cornered against a high ridge, without food. In search of a way out, the guerrillas ask an old friend (a missionary they had held hostage and released some 20 years ago) for the number of a humanitarian priest, in hopes of finding someone to bring food to the mountain. The missionary mistakes the priests' name for a head paramilitary leader, and inadvertently gives the guerrilla commanders the wrong number.

Through a humorous confusion, two sworn enemies end up face to face in an emotional encounter that unveils the very core of Colombia's conflict, and the journey each one must take to finally find peace in a lifetime of war.

Made in the USA
Columbia, SC
15 July 2024